JEEPERS CREEPERS

JEEPERS CREEPERS

Canadian Accounts of
Weird Events and Experiences

JOHN ROBERT COLOMBO

DUNDURN
TORONTO

Editor: Matt Baker
Design: Jesse Hooper
Printer: Webcom

Library and Archives Canada Cataloguing in Publication

Colombo, John Robert, 1936-
    Jeepers creepers : Canadian accounts of weird events
and experiences / John Robert Colombo.

Issued also in electronic formats.
ISBN 978-1-55488-976-1

    1. Curiosities and wonders--Canada. 2. Parapsychology--Canada. I. Title.

BF1472.C3C6555 2011   133.10971   C2011-902578-7

1   2   3   4   5   15   14   13   12   11

We acknowledge the support of the **Canada Council for the Arts** and the **Ontario Arts Council** for our publishing program. We also acknowledge the financial support of the **Government of Canada** through the **Canada Book Fund** and **Livres Canada Books**, and the **Government of Ontario** through the **Ontario Book Publishing Tax Credit** and the **Ontario Media Development Corporation**.

Printed and bound in Canada.
www.dundurn.com

Dundurn 3 Church Street, Suite 500 Toronto, Ontario, Canada M5E 1M2	Gazelle Book Services Limited White Cross Mills High Town, Lancaster, England LA1 4XS	Dundurn 2250 Military Road Tonawanda, NY U.S.A. 14150

Contents

PREFACE

In the pages of this book, you will find a goodly number of hair-raising stories concerning the supernatural. These are stories that tell us about ghosts and spirits, about events and experiences that are hard to believe — despite the fact that they have reportedly occurred. Indeed, they are "told as true." They are first-person accounts of the unexplained and possibly inexplicable. Reported to me by men and women from various parts of the country, these encounters are published in the words of the informants themselves, the witnesses to these wonders.

There are some thirty-five narratives in all, and they give us that many occasions and excuses to pause and wonder about the nature of reality, about life and death, and about the existence of alien entities and exotic dimensions of human experience. Here, you will have opportunities to read a lot about dreams and whether they are predictive or not; about whether when someone dies there is a spirit that survives the grave and remains in limited contact with the living; about strange goings-on in old houses that suggest either ghosts or poltergeists — noisy spirits that are still at large; about eerie coincidences that suggest the hand of destiny or the finger of fate! Such events and experiences are reported by reliable witnesses, all of them Canadians, responsible men and women who live in many parts of the country and are puzzled by what they have experienced.

This book is the latest of my collections — and perhaps the liveliest — in the long series of books that I have compiled that preserve accounts of Canadian encounters with the supernatural and the paranormal. It is titled *Jeepers Creepers*, a catchy title, because the contents of the book are lively and they express a certain degree of bafflement that is expressed in such terms as "Good Lord!" or "Oh, gosh!" or "Gee willikers!"

Indeed, the slang expression *jeepers creepers* dates back to the late 1920s. The editors of *The Oxford English Dictionary* suggest that the words are a corruption of the name of Jesus Christ. The words are recalled today because of the lyrics of the popular song of that name, a jazz favourite composed by Harry Warner and Johnny Mercer for the 1938 movie *Going Places*, starring Dick Powell and Ronald Reagan; I wonder which one of them was "the creeper." To calm down a restless racehorse, Louis Armstrong played the musical composition "Jeepers Creepers" on the trumpet! The movie is forgotten, but not the tune and the crazy words:

> Jeepers Creepers,
> where'd ya get those peepers?
> Jeepers Creepers,
> where'd ya get those eyes?

The question is easily asked, but never answered.

The following year, the character Porky Pig appeared as a ghost-hunter in the animated cartoon also called *Jeepers Creepers*, and the song was sung by the ghost in question, mainly to annoy Porky. This is how the expression came to be associated with ghosts. In 1983 a computer game was so named, but it was not for decades until a horror movie capitalized on the words. The movie *Jeepers Creepers* appeared in 2001; its sequel, *Jeepers Creepers II*, came (and went) in 2003; *Jeepers Creepers III* is scheduled to be released in 2013. These are not comedies but "slasher" movies. "The Creeper" is a mutant zombie-cockroach who eats the living bodies of high school basketball players and their girlfriends! The "creep" is a cockroach, all right, though most of the time he — or it — is dressed in regular business attire.

It occurred to me the words *jeepers creepers* might well be appropriated for more serious use and to serve as the title of a collection of ghost stories. Perhaps we should examine those words, too: *ghost stories*. In this book, the word *story* refers to a narrative that is true or is told-as-true.

What about the word *ghost*, and how does it differ from the word *spirit*? There is no hard-and-fast distinction between the two words or to what or to whom they refer, but the concepts are no less real for this ethereal quality, and common usage does provide some clues. Here is the way I like to distinguish between the words when I speak or write about mysterious subjects:

A *ghost* is what a person leaves behind after death; it once was a person.

A *spirit* is a power that is found to reside in a place or site.

Both ghosts and spirits are presences. The former presence, the ghost, may bear the name of a person whom you once knew. The latter presence, the spirit, is nameless but possesses potency or agency.

In practice we seldom make these rudimentary distinctions, yet it is useful to view supernatural and paranormal experiences, like hauntings or sightings, with such distinct presences as ghosts and spirits in mind. I will refer to ghost stories as "accounts of hauntings."

There are two types of hauntings and both of them are narrative accounts. There is the supernatural type, which is a traditional tale. Then there is the psychical or paranormal experience, which someone living or within living memory has experienced. It is told as true, whereas the traditional tale is a "jolly good story" — a yarn. Experiences of a supernatural nature and psychical events are felt to be inexplicable in natural terms, whereas parapsychological occurrences are held to be explainable.

The haunting of Edinburgh Castle in the Scottish capital is a supernatural tale, hoary with antiquity. The haunting of Mackenzie House is a reference to a series of psychical or paranormal experiences remembered by many people who live in Toronto today.

The playwright George Bernard Shaw was interested in ghost stories, and he once wrote a serious review of a book that collected traditional or supernatural ghost stories. In the review he made an amusing reference to "classical ghost stories." He began his sentence with these words: "Classical — therefore untrue — ghost stories ..."

There are also differences between the psychical and the paranormal, and while these differences are principally historical, they do have relevance today. Psychical events are activities that are set apart from scientific study, whereas the paranormal events are activity that is considered to be worthy of the study of scientists. At first, scientists and psychologists (and later sociologists and statisticians) were drawn to examine reports of anomalous experiences to find if they revealed patterns. The Society for Psychical Research was founded in England in 1880 by scientists, not psychics. The SPR examined psychical phenomena and sought to determine whether or not such activities existed, and if they did, whether they might be measured and objectively described. Members of the SPR, like members of its offshoot the American Society for Psychical Research (ASPR), were hard-headed physical scientists, though their ranks did included a few social psychologists like William James, who attended seances and examined "physical mediumship" (that is, the way mediums and psychics produce physical effects like table-tipping, trumpet-blowing, and oozing ectoplasm).

Parapsychological phenomena were the objects of study of J.B. Rhine, who founded the Parapsychological Laboratory at Duke University in Durham, North Carolina, in 1927. He sought to reproduce and measure mental effects that he called *psi* factors. These consisted of *psychokinesis* (moving objects at a distance), *telepathy* (reading minds), *clairvoyance* (seeing at a distance), *clairaudience* (hearing at a distance), and *precognition* (knowledge of the future). Rhine was a former biologist and his associates were largely experimental psychologists and statisticians who concentrated their efforts on examining "gifted people" with "special powers" who could predict or influence random-number generators against the law of averages.

In this way, the mystery of the seances migrated in the nineteenth century from the parlours of fashionable society to the research laboratories of major colleges and universities of the twentieth century. Today, there are private laboratories to study such phenomena, but a number of public universities — Princeton, Virginia, Arizona, Northampton, Liverpool, Edinburgh — have conducted or continue to conduct experiments and publish results in juried journals. The Koestler Parapsychology Unit within the Department of Psychology at the University of Edinburgh was endowed by the entire estate of the author Arthur Koestler upon his death in 1983.

It is relevant that the words *psychic* and *psychical* have different though related meanings. The former word refers to powers, and the latter refers to the study of those powers. A psychic, or spirit-medium, is someone gifted (or said to be gifted) with such powers. Research into those powers is psychical research, the modern term for which is *parapsychology*. The distinction is genuine, and the conventional wisdom today holds that what is psychical can never been substantiated to meet with scientific standards, but what is parapsychological may ultimately yield to scientific investigation. That distinction always brings to my mind the following interesting truism: "Superstition is superstition. But the study of superstition is science."

Often the reading public confuses literary ghost stories with real-life ghost stories. The former are the products of the literary imagination, though they may be inspired by traditional tales of a supernatural nature. Two outstanding practitioners of the art of writing literary ghost stories were Englishmen M.R. James (1862-1936), who was a don at Cambridge University, and Algernon Blackwood (1869-1951), a one-time journalist and later a full-time writer. (Blackwood is a particular favourite of mine; he lived in Toronto in the early 1880s.) James was the master of the antiquarian horror tale — ancient castles, ancient tomes, ancient spells, ancient forces — whereas Blackwood specialized in the tale of terror about evils as ancient as the Earth, like those identified today with the fiction of H.P. Lovecraft.

The Canadian writer who has made the liveliest and wittiest contribution to the literature of ghost stories is Robertson Davies (1913–1995), the novelist and playwright, who contributed thirteen "gaudies" (stories written as entertainments to be told each Christmas) set within the confines of Toronto's Massey College, where he served as its first master. His collection of these entertaining stories is called *High Spirits*. Unlike most writers who describe spooks and brutes, Master Davies, an erudite gentleman, demonstrated a light touch.

At one time or another, most serious novelists and short-story writers tackle the literary ghost story. I think immediately of Henry James's masterful short novel *The Turn of the Screw*, which is about a ghost that may be only a psychological obsession. (I should put the word "only" in quotation marks because that "only" is quite important in its own right.) Stories that describe seeing ghosts and sensing spirits are "as old as the hills" and they add another string to the writer's fiddle. From the earliest of times to the present day, literature has been rich in stories of ghosts and spirits, horrors and terrors, inexplicable events and eerie experiences, as well as descriptions of monstrous brutes and bizarre alien beings. Yet their present vogue may be said to be the handiwork of two people who influenced modern taste through their innumerable popular books of traditional and modern thrills and chills.

The name Andrew Lang (1844–1912) is familiar to students of folklore and legend. The Anglo-Scottish folklorist and writer published the so-called "coloured fairy books." There were titles like *The Blue Fairy Book*, *The Red Fairy Book*, and even *The Lilac Fairy Book*. In all, one dozen such titles appeared in print. Worse for the wear, copies of these volumes may be found on the bookshelves of summer cottages. Many people still living grew up with Lang's versions of traditional tales of hauntings. We owe to Lang our appreciation of the fairy lore of the land — "things that go bump in the night."

The name Elliott O'Donnell (1872–1965) is barely remembered today, but the Anglo-Irish journalist and editor was busy throughout much of the twentieth century, compiling and retelling his told-as-true stories of hauntings, creating a vogue for books like *Strange Disappearances* and *Strange Sea Mysteries*. Many of his "occult" stories convey what we know best about *ye olde* castles of Britain. So O'Donnell was a pioneer in collecting modern-day experiences of the weird sparked by old castles, mires, bogs, mountaintops, and so forth.

It is curious to realize that what we know about the nature of man and the workings of nature has been influenced by studies of ghosts and spirits in no small way. The ideas of two of the twentieth century's most influential thinkers, Sigmund Freud (1856–1939) and Carl Jung (1875–1961), are rooted in psychical research and parapsychology. For instance, Freud devoted his first and longest psychoanalytical study to a fictional character (who turns out to be simultaneously both real and imaginary) in his book-length study titled *Gradiva*. Freud once confessed, in a letter to his biographer Ernest Jones, "If I had my life to live over again, I would devote myself to psychical research rather than to psychoanalysis."

Jung was also intrigued with psychical research, especially with alchemy and other forms of occult thought and practice. His doctoral dissertation was on the secondary personality of a trance-medium who is known to this day as "Miss Frank Miller." She believed she channelled entities resident on the planet Mars. At both the beginning and the end of his life, Jung worked on a dissertation, which he initially titled

Psychology of the Unconscious and thereafter gave it more contemporary cachet by calling it *Symbols of Transformation*.

So both Freud and Jung were irresistibly drawn to occult thought, and it could be argued that they failed to keep a respectable distance from it. People might infer, then, that the subconscious is the realm of the repressed and the suppressed — ghosts. The collective unconscious is the domain of the archetypes — spirits. This formulation is a simple one, to be sure, but it does differentiate between the terms *ghosts* and *spirits*.

The leading contributors to psychical and parapsychological research in Canada were R.S. Lambert and A.R.G. Owen, with his wife Iris M. Owen. R.S. Lambert (1894–1981), known as "Rex," was a broadcaster and writer with BBC Radio in London, where he founded its famed periodical *The Listener*. He was the quintessential psychical researcher in Britain. He crossed the Atlantic Ocean in 1939, joined CBC Radio in Toronto, and served as superintendent of school broadcasts. He left his mark on this country with a beautifully written study called *Exploring the Supernatural: The Weird in Canadian Folklore*. On the one occasion that I met "Rex" Lambert, I was impressed with his integrity and his wide knowledge of mysterious matters.

Many times I met the other gentleman researcher, A.R.G. Owen (1919–2003), known as George, in the company of his delightful wife, Iris M. Owen (1916–2009), a social worker. The couple had lived in Cambridge, where George was a don and taught biostatistics. Before moving to Calgary, George joined the University of Toronto and the couple undertook parapsychological research. He wrote *Psychic Mysteries of Canada*, the second survey of the field, and Iris co-authored *Conjuring up Philip: A Study in Psychokinesis*, a landmark contribution to the dynamics of ideo-motor responses in group situations like seances.

Rex, George, and Iris inspired me to research, write, and publish a whole host of books in this field, beginning with

Mysterious Canada in 1979. Offbeat phenomena had always caught my eye, engaged my attention, and held my interest. I am especially appreciative of "the Canadian connections" with some of the best-known ghost stories and mysteries of all-time. Let me offer two instances: The greatest mystery of the sea concerns the *Mary Celeste*, the brigantine that was found abandoned on the high seas off the Azores. It turned out the brigantine was a Canadian-built vessel ... and a "jinxed" or "hoodoo" ship since its launch at Parrsboro, Nova Scotia. Similarly, the Modern Spiritualist movement of the nineteenth century generated worldwide interest. The two leading spiritualists of their day were uneducated farm girls, the Fox Sisters, born in Consecon, near Belleville, in Upper Canada, present-day Ontario. Maggie and Katie Fox moved with other members of their family to Hydesville, New York, where, in their farmhouse there, in 1847, they are credited with establishing two-way communication with "Mr. Splitfoot," a spirit of the dead. Today, the Fox Sisters are recognized to be the founders of the Modern Spiritualist movement.

One of the world's leading psychologists was William James, brother of the novelist Henry James. He was also an active parapsychologist, a notable philosopher, a founder of the philosophical movement known as Pragmatism, and a student of mystical states of mind. He wrote the standard book on that subject, *The Varieties of Religious Experience*, which consists of a series of lectures that have stood the test of time, despite the fact that the series was published way back in 1902. One of the ornaments of Harvard University, he found time to serve as president of both the Society for Psychical Research in England and the American Society for Psychical Research. In later life, he boasted that he had devoted twenty-five years to studying mediumship, clair-voyance, clairaudience, psychokinesis, and related phe-nomena. He marvelled that he felt he had made little or no progress, even after a quarter-century of investigation and experimentation in these fields, attending seances in parlours and theatres and attending to the needs of individual psychics and mediums. He expressed puzzlement about this in the essay that he called "The Final Impressions of a Psychical Researcher" (1909), available in *William James on Psychical Research* (1960), edited by Gardner Murphy and Robert O. Ballou. Here is what he confessed:

> Yet I am theoretically no "further" than I was at the beginning; and I confess that at times I have been tempted to believe that the Creator has eternally intended this department of nature to remain *baffling*, to prompt our curiosities and hopes and suspicions in all equal measure, so that, although ghosts and clairvoyances, and raps, and messages from spirits, are always seeming to exist and can never be fully explained away, they also can never be susceptible of full collaboration.

Yet, James, far from abandoning this field for the richer rewards of psychology and philosophy, continued to cultivate his connections, frequently consulting a medium who he called Mrs. Piper. Over many years, she confided details about his personal life to him that he felt that she had no way of knowing — and really no right to know. He marvelled at this knowledge and had no explanation for Mrs. Piper's access to it. Deeply puzzled by her mediumistic abilities, he called her his "white crow." Indeed, he wrote, "If you wish to upset the law that all crows are black, it is enough if you prove that one crow is white. My white crow is Mrs. Piper." Eventually, he came to the conclusion that Mrs. Piper's ability was not unique. In the essay "What Psychical Research Has Accomplished" (1897), he argued that experiences of psychics and their patrons, far from being remarkable, are really quite common:

The first difference between the psychical researcher and the inexpert person is that the former realizes the commonness and typicality of the phenomenon here, while the latter, less informed, thinks it is so rare as to be unworthy of attention. *I wish to go on record for the commonness.*

No one could ever convince James that Mrs. Piper was a fraudulent trance medium, but at the same time, he found it hard to believe that she was a genuine trance medium. James resembles the rest of us — having a divided soul.

With this in mind, perhaps *Jeepers Creepers* is as much a book about haunted Canadians as it is about Canadian hauntings.

Haunted sites and oddities are found right across the country. The Atlantic provinces are rich in phantom ships, spectral vessels, and "Grey Ladies," who stalk the seashores in search of their drowned children. Quebec has haunted residences and churches with miraculous healing statues. Ontario has innumerable farmhouses that serve as the loci of poltergeist-like effects. The Prairie provinces are the domain of the Windigo and mysterious medicine wheels. The West Coast's interior is the home of the sasquatch and Ogopogo, and the coastal areas are the breeding-grounds of other fabulous, aquatic creatures. The lands of the North have peculiar cairns and inukshuks; Sedna is the all-powerful denizen of the waters of the North, responsible for choppy seas and stormy weather. Indeed, the most mysterious place in the entire country (and perhaps in the entire world) is the North Pole.

No one can collect ghosts, but everyone can collect ghost stories, and over the years I have amassed close to one thousand of them. I scour the columns of old newspapers and periodicals on the lookout for supernatural tales. I encourage people I meet at my talks or on the street to send me written accounts of any odd and unusual experiences that they have had, as long as these are suitable for publication. These written accounts I call *memorates*.

The word *memorate* is used by folklorists to refer to a told-as-true narrative account of a peculiar event or experience that is related to close friends, not to the world at large. The fact that these "tellings" are meant for limited circulation is an important feature of the memorate, because there are things we tell family members and friends that we do not necessarily tell anyone else, certainly not total strangers.

No sooner had I begun to collect these memorates than I started to notice that, regardless of their contents, they have one characteristic form consisting of three parts. The first part is the introduction, which basically says, "You won't believe what I'm going to tell you." This is rarely hyperbole. The second part is the story itself, the body of the account, and it tells, in a little or a lot of detail, depending on the informant and the listeners, what the informant says has happened to him or to her. The third part is the closing, which basically says, "I don't know what to make of this." In other words, the informant is admitting that he or she does not know what has happened. In fact, not all that many people believe in the existence of ghosts and spirits, certainly not everyone who claims to have experienced their presence. The greatest skeptics are sometimes those people who report anomalous experiences like these and then maintain they do not know what to make of them!

What I have always found surprising is that an informant, depending on age, will recall, with great excitement and clarity of detail, an event or an experience that took place ten, twenty, forty, or even sixty years earlier, despite the fact that the duration of the experience may have been no more than a minute or two. It is difficult to account for the physiological, emotional, and intellectual responses to such experiences, not to mention their persistence in memory.

I am regularly asked, "Do you believe in ghosts?" I generally respond, "I do not believe in ghosts, I do not disbelieve in ghosts, I am *interested* in ghosts." If the questioner persists, I might reply, "Ghosts and spirits do not belong to the category of belief, but to the category of *experience*." Over the last half-century of reading and amassing accounts like these, I have come to three conclusions with respect to reports of encounters with ghosts and spirits.

The first conclusion is the simple fact that such encounters (like the ones in the present collection) have been reported in all cultures at all times. Rather than being uncommon, these experiences are quite common. There was a time when they were discussed in psychology textbooks in the section near the end titled "Abnormal Psychology." That is not the case today, for they are analyzed in a section that is reserved for "Anomalous Experiences." Indeed, the term *anomalous experience* was coined, or at least given wide currency, by Graham Reed, a psychologist at York University. In his study *The Psychology of Anomalous Experience*, published in 1988, he noted, "Every time one person is reported as having seen a ghost or a flying saucer, a crowd of others suddenly 'remember' that they too witnessed the phenomenon."

The second conclusion is that these reports about ghosts and spirits do not necessarily tell us anything about the afterlife. Views about life after death are subsumed under the title "the survival hypothesis," the notion that following physical death some portions of our being, psyche, spirit, vitality, or soul remains around, in some ways detectable, in other ways undetectable. In the same manner, reports of flying saucers or unidentified flying objects tell us nothing about life on other planets, in our own solar system, or in remote solar systems. This is known as "the extraterrestrial hypothesis," the notion that there is intelligent life on distant planets or in other dimensions of existence.

The third conclusion that I came to is that the human species has a special feeling for "mysteries" and that it comprises a small but important part of our personality and being. I like to recall one of Marshall McLuhan's statements: "The most human thing about man is his technology." It sounds paradoxical but it is strictly true. In that vein, let me add that "the most human thing about man is his interest in ghosts and spirits." We know of no other species that exhibits such an interest and concern.

Why are we concerned about the supernatural and the paranormal? I think there are three reasons why these matters absorb and enthrall us.

First, we enjoy a good story. Ghost stories, whether supernatural or parapsychological in nature, are gripping. After we hear about a haunting, especially one that involves someone we know and trust, we find ourselves wondering, "Can this be true? Do such things happen? Is there no other explanation?"

Second, we enjoy a good puzzle or mystery. We enjoy trying to resolve a complication, often forgetting that while a puzzle may be solved (it is a matter of rearranging the pieces), a mystery is never solved (it is a matter of missing or overlapping pieces). Samuel Boswell, the biographer, used to irritate the lexicographer and essayist Dr. Samuel Johnson by asking him to admit to a belief in ghosts. Dr. Johnson would have none of it. "It is wonderful that five thousand years have now elapsed since the creation of the world, and still it is undecided whether or not there has ever been an instance of the spirit of any person appearing after death. All argument is against it; but all belief is for it." So I think not only is mankind divided on the issue of the existence of ghosts and spirits, each one of us is divided on this subject too.

Third, as a species, we are curious about life — both human life and life in all its forms on earth, as well as possible existence before and after life. We have the vague sense that there is knowledge to be acquired here about human nature, if not about the nature of life itself.

So, all in all, I feel that the study of ghosts, spirits, and our obsessions with them is a positive undertaking and not a limiting one. I like to say, "ghosts are good for us," because they encourage us to probe and ponder. They also permit us — without embarrassment — to use such words as afterlife, being, destiny, essence, fate, fortune, karma, kismet, life, lot, predestination, psyche, reincarnation, soul, and spirit.

My feeling is that a sense of the mysterious lies at the heart of our existence and informs the spirit of our endurance as a species. While that sense may be the source of some of our delusions, it may just as well expand our horizons through the arts and the sciences. We know much about the physics of the everyday world, yet there is so much more to learn about human nature, especially expectation and rational explanation.

Whenever I entertain thoughts like these, I want to pull back from the brink. I remember the remarkable words of Joseph Conrad. In his ominously titled novella, *The Shadow Line: A Confession* (1917), the Polish-born English novelist showed his hand when he focused his attention on the actions of men and women rather than, like his fellow novelist Henry James, on the possible motivations behind these actions. He found the known world to be even more fascinating than the unknown world. I will allow Conrad the final words:

> The world of the living contains enough marvels and mysteries as it is — marvels and mysteries acting upon our emotions and intelligence in ways so inexplicable that it would almost justify the conception of life as an enchanted state. No, I am too firm in my consciousness of the marvellous to be ever fascinated by the mere supernatural which (take it any way you like) is but a manufactured article, the fabrication of minds insensitive to the intimate delicacies of our relation to the dead and to the living, in

their countless multitudes; a desecration of our tenderest memories; an outrage on our dignity.

Acknowledgements

"Of the making of books there is no end," observed King Solomon. How right he was and is! I am indebted to a great many men and women for so generously sharing their insights and experiences with me in "the making of books." For decades I was assisted in my ongoing researches by the late Mary Alice Neal, a friend of long-standing. Along the way, I have benefitted from the well-honed research skills of friend and librarian Philip Singer. Tony Hawke, another friend, was there to publish many of my early books. The present work was seen through the press by Michael Carroll of Dundurn, the remarkably resilient and well-rounded publishing house under the command of Kirk Howard and Beth Bruder (known in the trade as "Captain Kirk" and "Comrade Beth"). It was edited by Matt Baker and designed by Jesse Hooper. Independent researchers who have contributed to past books of mine include E. Ritchie Benedict, Edward Butts, and Dwight Whalen. Contributions were also made by Denise Bonds and Christian R. Page, mainstays of the television series *Dossiers mystère* (*Missing Link*), who have set a high benchmark for coverage of mysteries on Canadian television. Matthew James Didier founded the Toronto Ghosts and Hauntings Research Society in 1997, and the organization has raised the bar for the reporting of strange encounters. I have enjoyed a good many discussions about traditional motifs, mainstream mysteries, and dream imagery with the late Edith Fowke as well as with Ted Davy, James George, Cyril Greenland, David A. Gotlib, and Ted Mann. Technical assistance was supplied by Frank Spitzer, George A. Vanderburgh, and Bill Andersen.

My wife, Ruth Colombo, offered many a constructive comment along the way. Inevitably, my greatest debt is due to the contributors to the present collection, as well as to the contributors to past collections and, I hope, to the contributors to future collections of accounts of those remarkable experiences that do happen to responsible and sensible people.

This Happened to Me This Week

Ray Amell

I received a quite interesting email from Ray Amell, a reader of my books who lives in Brockville, Ontario. It was dated August 27, 2009, and it concerned a series of serendipitous events about a genealogical search and headstones in graveyards. I was intrigued. Here is what Mr. Amell wrote:

Mr. Colombo,

I have just read *True Canadian Ghost Stories* and enjoyed it very much. Am looking forward to getting a copy of *The Big Book of Canadian Ghost Stories* this week, here in Brockville.

I don't know if you are still collecting unusual stories, but this week my wife and I experienced an unusual happening while researching her family tree, looking for headstones on Alumette Island in the Pontiac region of Quebec, across the river from Pembroke, Ontario.

I have written a short sequence of events and would share it with you if you are still collecting such stories. Basically, I have been researching the Howard and Amell families and collecting information on the web, speaking to family members as well as visiting old cemeteries. We (my wife Kathleen and I) visited the cemetery in St. Joseph Parish on the Island this week and found the lost grave marker of my wife's grandparents (Howard) by a very strange sequence of events. The incident occurred on day special to a family member who had passed away. The Howards had migrated from Ireland during the potato famine in 1845–46 and settled on the Island.

If you are still collecting, let me know and I will forward my story to you

Naturally, I responded to Mr. Amell right away, assuring him that I was still collecting ghost stories and asking him to send me his account. When it arrived the next day, it bore the title "This Happened to Me This Week, Aug. 25, 2009."

His account will be of particular interest to everyone who has conducted research, especially genealogical research. Incidents like the coincidences described here do happen, and they happen quite often, so often, in fact, that the Swiss psychologist Carl Jung created a term to describe them. He called such incidents synchronicities — events with no known or possible causal relationship that do occur and seem to be more than casual! Coincidence? Good luck? Happy chance? The luck of the Irish?

Believe it or not, this is how it happened.

This week we were in Pembroke and Alumette Island, in the Pontiac region of Quebec where the Howard clan settled after their arrival in Canada about 1846. I was searching for the grave marker of Thomas and Bridget Howard in St. Joseph Parish on the Island.

I had searched the web on *ancestry.ca* and other sites for old headstones marking graves of Howard and Amell ancestries. The headstone I found was labelled "Howard" — Thomas and Bridget and sons Patrick and Maurice. It was labelled as being in St. Joseph Cemetery in St. Joseph Parish.

On Monday we arrived on the Island and visited the St. Joseph Cemetery in the company of one of Kathleen's relatives — Donna T., who lives near the graveyard and St. Joseph Parish Church.

I took several photographs of a number of headstones that Donna pointed out for my family-tree project.

I asked about a headstone for "Thomas and Bridget." Donna said that she had never seen one in that cemetery or in any other cemetery on the Island. I showed her the picture from the Net and she was amazed that it existed. After an extensive search of every marker in the cemetery, with no luck, we left for the day.

On Tuesday morning, August 25, we visited the other cemetery. This one is in Chapeau at the other end of island, at St-Alphonse-de-Liguori Church. I took several other photos but still we had no luck locating the Thomas / Bridget stone.

That afternoon, I visited the office in Pembroke of the Upper Ottawa Valley Genealogical Group. We searched their records much of the afternoon, and I collected and verified some valuable information for my family-tree project. Before we left, I mentioned to one of the folks at the centre that I was searching for this particular headstone. I showed them the picture I had from the Net.

They looked up some old records from the St. Joseph Cemetery and found an entry that matched the names I was looking for. They had surveyed the cemetery some time ago and had recorded listings of various headstones. Finally, after a bit of searching, they told me, "Yes there is a grave there and it is somewhere near the markers for 'Cosgrove' and 'Duff.'" They were "somewhere in the cemetery."

Okay. So we would have to go back and look again. Well, we did. Sure enough, there were the two markers of Cosgrove and Duff. There was nothing but green grass between or near them.

I had a metal detector with me. Out of curiosity, trusting my luck, I walked the area with a very slight hope that I may pick up "something" that might have been put there with metal in or with it at some time in the past. No luck.

Okay, now comes the part I want to put on paper. Kay witnessed the whole episode.

I started walking from the Duff marker toward the Cosgrove marker. They were about fifty feet apart. About fifteen feet from the Duff marker, I stopped. I didn't know why. There was nothing there but grass. There was a fence nearby.

Something made me stop. It did so not in words, but in thought. For some reason I knelt down and pulled out my pocket knife. It has a three and one-half inch long blade. I started to push it into the ground.

On the second push, it struck something solid. My knife blade scraped it. It felt like I was scratching stone. There was a screeching sound of metal on stone. I started cutting away the sod, which was about three or four inches deep. As I cut away, I could see the top of a flat red-granite headstone as it was being exposed. I kept cutting the sod away, and what was gradually revealed was the headstone of Thomas and Bridget Howard with a notation: "and their sons, Patrick and Maurice."

Kay just stood there and couldn't believe what had happened.

I uncovered the complete stone, exposing the writing, and washed it off. It was the stone we were looking for. Identical to photo I had copied from the Web but hidden under a layer of sod and grass so that it was not visible above ground.

Thomas and Bridget were Joseph Francis Howard's parents. (Maurice and Patrick were two of his brothers.) This would have been Joe's 107th. (He had been born on August 25, 1902.)

Is it not odd that I found his parents' headstone on his 107th birthday, to the day, in the way that I did?

I'm sure everyone will have his or her own explanation for this one! My own explanation is that it was a cross inter-dimensional / time experience at its best. This is not an exaggeration in any way, and it happened exactly as I have described it.

Her only comment, as she stood there, was, "Thank you, Joe, and have a happy birthday."

If you look closely at the picture with the overturned sod exposed, you can see the reverse imprint of the marker writing embedded in the bottom side of the sod that I had removed.

My Other Ghostly Experience

Ann Atherstone

The author of the following email is a woman I have never met but would one day like to. A few years ago, she sent me a finely written account of her eerie experience. I accepted it for publication in my next collection and wrote to her to this effect. It duly appeared in *The Big Book of Canadian Ghost Stories*. Although it appeared, somehow her mailing and emailing addresses both *disappeared*. (That sounds like an unlikely mystery story: "The Case of the Disappearing Addresses"!) Luckily for both of us, Ms. Genders kept in touch and sent me a query about the fate of her account. I was relieved that I was able to send her a copy of the book. In my letter promising her a copy of the collection, I asked if the experience she had described was an isolated one. Anticipating the delivery of the long-delayed copy, she sent me the following list of odd occurrences that had "come her way" over the years.

I will now let Ms. Genders continue in her own lively way.

Thank you for your kind letter, John. I will look forward to the book. Yes, I have had other incidents, having noticed "strange" things all of my life, but most of them have been more of a mystical nature, and not ghostly.

Though as college students living on Sandford Avenue, my roommate and I sincerely believed the house we lived in was being attended to by the deceased husband of the lady from whom we were renting our flat. A widow of long-standing, she was nevertheless very happy and felt he was around somehow. We noticed that whenever we wanted to go out and party, our keys or change purses would disappear. This occurred so frequently that we had to plan how to get back into the house "after curfew" without our keys, which we would find in very odd places the next day (e.g., in a flour bin).

Regarding other types of supernatural incidents....

I have seen my father ... he appeared in his housecoat, but only from the mid-thighs down — I knew the housecoat, his legs, and his hammer toes.

I have had the family dog wake me up whining to be let out — from hundreds of miles away — and phoned home to no answer, only to learn later that my parents had been to an out-of-town wedding, and that the dog had not been able to hold herself until they got back home.

Once, my small son and I were at one end of my long, wide dresser. He was watching me brush my hair, when suddenly at the other end, bobby pins and rubber bands literally threw themselves across the room; this did upset my son, and I had to assure him I knew he did not do it, as I saw the whole explosion.

And, as a young homemaker, I knew exactly which friend or relative was calling me when the phone rang, or that it was a stranger, and friends referred to me as psychic because of my accuracy. Years of working in offices since then seems to have dulled that ability!

I have heard some amazing experiences from other people, too, such as NDEs [near death experiences], but regarding the ghostly....

My best friend in high school sometimes saw an Indian man, at times in full regalia, sitting cross-legged in her basement on the floor. He never spoke, never smiled. She herself was a very cheery person, not given to depressing topics of conversation, so what was interesting to me was that she thought they had built her house over a native burial site. What's more, she later experienced the death of her beloved teenaged cousin and her father by the time she was eighteen. The odds of two such deaths occurring being very low in our experience, might the apparition be seen as a harbinger on the one hand, or a comfort on the other? She was adopted, and we had little information on her heritage.

Another friend was babysitting a late evening for her sister, so was staying the night at her sister's new house, which had been previously owned by a couple now divorced. She thought she heard her sister coming home so she came out of her room to the top of the landing, where she could see the front door. Her sister was not there, but there was a single pair of feet dancing in a beam of moonlight, wearing red high heels with a strap, from the fifties. It really freaked her, as she was not the type given to fanciful notions.

In the seventies, there was a ghost that liked to push and once even punched a friend's wife whenever they sat at the kitchen table at her sister-in-law's on Lippincott Avenue. She thought it was her husband doing it and that everyone else was trying to put one over on her, until one time she had pulled her chair away from the table and could see everyone — that was the time "Harry," as they had come to call him, punched her quite hard.

Another very weird incident involved my husband and his two sisters, who were once visiting a relative to attend a funeral and sitting in the basement talking. They had a suitcase with them, which suddenly opened and the contents flew out. This was upsetting to them, as none of them were close to the suitcase, but it was something they revisited often when they got together, and obviously not a fun tale for them.

However, *my* other personal ghostly experience of note follows.

One very active house we lived in was just north of Dufferin Park on the 400 block of Gladstone Avenue, in Toronto. Through the early 1980s, the three-storey, five-bedroom house was occupied by my husband and me, our two small children, our teen-aged niece, and a friend of long-standing who was rooming with us.

First we would hear footsteps coming up the stairs and going down the hall of the second floor, to the back of the house where there was a sun room in which we had a small painting studio. There was a large bedroom with bay windows in the front, where our niece had her room, then our room, a very large bathroom, and the sun room. Because no one really used the studio except me, we were always looking for whoever was going into the room. The footsteps sounded like those of an adult, but I would check, not wanting the kids to get into mischief.

About six weeks after moving in, we heard the footsteps coming up the stairs while both my husband and I were talking in our room with the door wide open. We looked as we heard the steps approach our door, thinking it was our roomer, but no one appeared. We were dumfounded that the sounds continued down the hall. That was when we realized this was not some acoustic anomaly, but a ghost. Not only was it able to make the sound of footsteps, but one day while coming down the stairs, I heard someone at the front door, which was inside an overhang on the veranda, with a large panel of plain glass. I couldn't see anyone at the door, and the vantage point I had at the top of the stairs was such that I could see there were no little kids hunched up behind the door, but the heavy crystal knob kept turning. After it stopped, I went down to make sure no one was there, and I was right.

Then one of the kids mentioned seeing an old man sitting in their room on the third floor, looking a bit sad, who they described as wearing a white shirt, grey pants, and suspenders. He was just sitting there on the bed along the south wall, then not there. Though it didn't bother them (they were just grabbing some toys), of course this concerned me.

Very close to that time, my niece began experiencing very bad dreams, often waking up feeling that *someone* was sitting on her chest, once even trying to strangle her. I should say that her room was not inviting, somehow, as was the rest of the house, and no one liked to be in it for very long. Our boarder perceived there to be a cold mist in her room one evening when she was afraid to go to bed, and I asked her about the picture by the side of her bed. It was an old photograph of her grandparents; her prim grandfather had been depressed, got arrested for drunkenness, which was very unusual for him, and subsequently hanged himself. The friend suggested she put away the photograph, we said some prayers together in the room, and that seemed to put an end to her problem.

The footsteps continued, however, but we saw no more movements of doorknobs or people out of place in the house, which we moved out of in 1983.

Someone Gasping for Air

M. Marlene Beyer

This chatty email arrived on June 14, 2009. I read it with interest because it had come from the personal computer of M. Marlene Beyer, a valued contributor to one of my earlier collections of eerie tales, *The Big Book of Canadian Ghost Stories*.

The present short account consists of a series of odd occurrences — impressions of domestic details rather than perceptions of good or evil, or conceptions of a grand nature. By their very nature, impressions are subjective rather than substantial, but are nonetheless real.

It is difficult to know what to make of Ms. Beyer's account of her experiences, other than to conclude that she is a sensitive woman and perhaps has a "psychic streak." No matter where she lives, she senses unusual events and has unusual experiences! Some people are like that....

Good evening, John,

I've had some interesting life changes during the last four months that have found me in Woodstock, Ontario.

I have moved into what was Broadway Public School and what is now a condominium complex. The original school was built in the late 1800s and a "new" addition was added in the early 1900s (the part that I now reside in). My condo is in what was once the school's auditorium and gymnasium.

When I initially moved in, I was unaware of the school's history or what part of the building my unit had originally been.

About a month later, I was awoken by (what appeared to be) the rapid breathing of my cat, close to my face. Concerned, I went to place my hand on the cat, only to discover that I was "alone" in my bedroom, my cat sleeping by the fireplace in the living room.

On another night, I awoke to the sound of a ball being bounced up and down (in what sounded like) my living room. Thinking that it might be one of the children in the building, I began to get out of my bed and the sound ceased.

Quite recently, my daughter, Aryme, spent a week with me after graduating from teacher's college. One evening, I had a vivid dream that I had been pulled into an undertow and that I was drowning. The dream was so vivid, in fact, that it woke me. In the morning, I noticed that my hall closet was opened and that there were several items of winter clothing on the floor (this happened in June). Upon further inspection, I realized that my "Mustang" life jacket had inflated! This type of jacket is designed not to deploy until it is immersed in (approximately) a metre of water.

Later that morning, I called my daughter; when I asked her about her night, she stated that she had not slept well and that she had heard "the sound of a dog panting" in the night. When I questioned her further, she stated that the "sound" could have sounded like "someone gasping for air."

I'll leave it to you, John, to decide.

In a subsequent exchange of emails, Ms. Beyer responded in these words to my suggestion that she is psychic. After reading of her experiences, I am doubly certain that she possesses a "psychic streak"!

I don't know whether I have a "psychic streak" as you mentioned; perhaps it is more the ability to perceive sadness or distress in others, from whichever plane of existence. I forgot to tell you that, about two months ago, I managed to actually fall quite soundly asleep (I am a chronic insomniac), when I was abruptly awoken by the sound of a ball being thrown and bouncing off the outside wall of my condo. Since it was after 11:00 p.m., I figured that some neighbourhood children were trying to break my window. I scrambled out of bed, armed with enough profanity to (hopefully) frighten them away. The banging on the wall continued until the *moment* I reached the window, and then it abruptly stopped. With the assistance of an (almost) full moon and the street lights, I had a fairly good view of the yard, but could see no one and heard no footsteps. It was the following day that I discovered that I was currently residing in what was once the school's gymnasium.

My initial interaction with "Broadway School" occurred shortly before I ever moved in. On a bright, wintry morning in February, I decided to drive past the school. As I was leaving, I glanced up into the bell tower and saw (what appeared to me to be) an elderly, balding gentleman, methodically cleaning the tower windows. As I mentioned, it was a bright winter morning and we must have stared at one another for over five minutes. Eventually realizing how rude I was being, I waved at him, but he did not return my greeting. The following week, I enquired about the gentleman who was living in the bell tower. When I asked for his description, I was told that he was in his *late twenties*, with dark hair. I have since met this young man's father, who in no way resembles the image I witnessed for over five minutes on that morning in February.

I must admit, that as sad as I have been, I feel quite comfortable with the residents (alive or otherwise) who reside in and continue to attend Broadway Public School. I am attempting to gain some knowledge as to the history of the school.

My Story and Its Aftermath

Janet Brown

"I received this email from Janet Brown, a correspondent who was otherwise unknown to me."

So began the note that I wrote to introduce Janet Brown's account of multiple weird experiences that she had in 1968, when she was a teenager. She described her experiences in four parts with a brief introduction and a longer conclusion. They involved members of her family in their home in Windsor, Ontario, and at a cottage on Prince Edward Island. I will not describe those experiences here, because they are quite detailed and may be found in full in my collection titled *Strange but True*, which was published in 2007. Suffice to say, these strange psychical experiences seem to be part of Mrs. Brown's life.

Three years later, I received an email from Mrs. Brown in late February 2010, offering to correct the street address of the family home. I responded by asking Mrs. Brown if she had experienced any other odd moments in her later residences. She replied in the affirmative, so I encouraged her to type them up and to send them to me.

She has now done so. I am including her interesting account, and though I have suppressed the two street addresses mentioned in the first paragraph I have kept the street name. There is no need to frighten subsequent occupants of the houses in question!

Hi, Mr. Colombo:

At your suggestion I am writing to make a correction concerning the account of "My Story" that you kindly included in your book titled *Strange but True*. The address of the house I lived in was not [removed] Esdras Place but rather [removed] Esdras Place in Windsor, Ontario.

I was a young girl at that time and believed that I was experiencing a haunting connected to my late uncle. Years later I questioned all the past conclusions I had come to as my father revealed that the house was indeed "known to be haunted." In a quest to once again decide if it was indeed my uncle, I admit that even today, some forty-two years later, I am uncertain. I do know that although nothing nearly as intense as what happened at that time has occurred over the years, many isolated and unexplainable things have taken place. I did recount a few of these in the previous story. However, I will include here the incidents that have taken place in the home we now live in.

We moved to my husband's hometown of Peterborough, Ontario, in 1987. At that time, our son Jason was fifteen and our daughter Shannon was eleven. Neither one was very impressed with this old house. The house this year is one hundred years old. We've worked on it and made it a home that we now enjoy, with visits from grandchildren as well.

I will add that as a family we are quite down to earth and attempt to be "good Catholics." Early on, Jason purchased an Ouija board and spent a considerable amount of time in his room with his friends playing with it. One day he shared that there were spirits speaking to him through the board, claiming to be my husband's recently deceased father. He lamented that at first he thought it was "cool," but that it had scared him terribly by saying it wanted to possess him. At that same time, Shannon fell down the stairs carrying a pair of scissors. There was a very tangible bad feeling in our home. We got rid of the board and things eventually seemed to go back to normal.

Some time later, Shannon had a very bad experience. My husband and I were up late watching a movie. She came tearing downstairs from her room and told us that, while completely awake, she saw a black form with hands extended on her bedroom floor beside her bed. We took it very seriously and decided to call in a priest to bless the house. To this day, Shannon simply states that "you're never alone here." Her husband, also named Jason, claims to feel it too. Our son, who is very spiritual, takes it a step further. He has shared with me that he doesn't like to be alone here. He claims that it doesn't feel like a "good" spirit. I on the other hand can say that I also never feel alone, but I now believe it is a spirit that is attached to me. I don't feel that it is "bad" but oddly enough has actually given me comfort at times. I surmise that this is because it has been with me so very long. In the years to follow, little odd happenings have occurred, minor things that I believe we all experience. An example would be the jingling of the light cord at the top of the stairs leading to the basement, heard clearly by me from the living room while at home alone. Another would be one day last summer, returning home from being away for several days. I walked in to the kitchen and heard very clearly a deep sigh that came from the living room....

Also, approximately three months ago, I was standing at my kitchen sink doing dishes. Ron was sitting to my right, in the rocking chair reading. To my left and directly across from Ron is a small TV. I was enjoying the quiet, as Ron, to my annoyance, tends to turn the TV on more then I'd like. I heard very clearly a pretty little tune playing. I reacted negatively but thought better than to say anything. All this took place in a very short period of time. When I turned to the TV to see what was on, I realized it was not turned on at all....

More substantial is the following account, which I wrote in 2007: Approximately ten months ago my husband started a new job out of town. He lived and worked away from home for the next five months. Now, as I've previously stated, I always feel quite at ease here at home, so the incident I am about to relate came as quite a surprise. However, it did not "scare" me as much as I would have thought.

We had gotten up early the morning my husband left. It was about 10:00 a.m. when he got on his way. I've never been much of a morning person, and as I didn't have anything pressing to keep me up, I decided to take a nap. My bedroom is rather bright, so I choose to nap in the basement. It is almost pitch-black down there and very comfortable. My husband had it set up that way when he worked nights.

While I had just settled in and was lying there in the dark, I heard, to my amazement, the faint yet unmistakable strum of a guitar! I kept my cool and tried to rationalize how this was possible. I then remembered that there was indeed a guitar resting against a corner wall. My brother had given it to my husband several years ago. My husband didn't play, but even so it was a source of entertainment to try for the couple of times he picked it up. It had been in that corner for a long time since. I finally decided to turn on the light to gather my bearings. I did so. Several minutes later I thought, "this is silly." I then turned the light out, and sure enough, several seconds later I heard the strum once again! I swore and jumped out of the bed, more annoyed at the disturbance of my nap than scared.

I am beginning to accept the fact that we are probably not alone here. Seemingly there is no malice.

My brother who gave my husband the guitar passed away in August. His loving and heartbroken wife claims he has visited her. He was a firm believer in the afterlife and I'm sure if there were a way to come back he would. They say that as we get older we become more childlike. I believe that is true. We become more aware and accepting of the reality that is as fascinating as it is incredible!

The last experience I put to paper I will admit left me quite unnerved. This happened a short while ago. Our bedroom is on the third floor of our home, and the second floor is furnished but unoccupied. This includes our daughter Shannon's old room. I point this out, because as you can imagine, as a parent of a teenaged girl I slept regularly with one ear open and still do. (I could hear her door open the exact moment that it did.) I have never in general been a sound sleeper.

However, to continue, one night while sleeping, I distinctly heard a sound like someone at the foot of the stairs rubbing up against our bedroom door. As I suddenly awoke, I heard the noise for the second time. I quickly sat up at complete attention. My husband, although hard of hearing, was startled awake by my movement. I told him what I'd heard, and he asked, "So you think there is someone in the house?" I said that I did. He got up and checked, but there was no one to be found.... Just when I've convinced myself that there is nothing here.... Well....

This concludes my experiences up to this point. I very much appreciate the forum to allow me to share this with others, who I hope won't judge my sanity.

Thanks so much for your time and support.

P.S. I intended but decided not to leave this out.

Several years ago, my husband and I went to see a young Catholic girl who claimed to see guardian angels. A priest in our diocese had brought her here to Peterborough. There was a long line up in the small hall to see her. My husband was several people ahead of me. I had only decided at the last minute to go up. He came back, beaming, to tell me she'd told him his angel's name was David and that he was the largest angel she'd ever seen. She also laughed that David had a great sense of humour. I didn't really know what to think but was interested in what she would say to me. To my surprise and confusion, she did not react well to me. It was more her body language and the feeling that she just wanted me to move on. I don't recall what was said. I am a very perceptive person and easily empathize with people. My husband didn't see any problem but it has always bothered me. I often wonder what put her off....

"I'm All Right, Joanne!"

Joanne Doyle

I received this charmingly written email on May 7, 2010. It had been posted to me some days earlier, but it arrived while I was out of town. Nevertheless, I am pleased to have received it and I want to thank Mrs. Doyle for writing it.

We often dream of loved ones after they have died. When this happens, the overall message of the dream is usually that everything is now fine: there is no need to worry. That is certainly the case in this instance. There is no proof that there is survival after physical death, yet there are so many accounts of the deceased communicating with the living, it is foolish to simply dismiss the possibility of "spirit communication" out of hand.

Mrs. Doyle is of two minds about what is going on here, and I expect that readers of this account will agree with her. I find the experience she recounts to be a testimonial to the power of love ... a power that may well be more enduring than death itself.

Dear Mr. Colombo,

I have always been interested in paranormal occurrences, ghosts, and hauntings, and have found your books very interesting, especially the accounts of hauntings in areas where I have lived. The following story is about my father-in-law, his death, and the message I received after his death.

My husband, myself, and our three children were living in a small community called Kendal. We had built a house and were very happy living in the country. My father-in-law, Leo, had just retired, and he and my mother-in-law built an addition to our home and had moved in. It wasn't very long before he became ill and was subsequently diagnosed with a rare and terminal form of leukemia. He lasted through two bouts of chemo, but that only bought him a year. He decided to be at home when the time came, and all of his children were there to send him off. He even waited until his daughter arrived from Ottawa, then he just took a breath and died.

I have always been close to Leo. He was an exceptional man, greatly loved by all. After the funeral was over, and everyone had to go on with life, I had a hard time coping with the idea of him being all right in his new appointment, and often lay awake wondering this thought. Finally, after weeks of unrest, I asked, one night in prayer, "Leo, I just want to know if you're okay."

That night, I had a wonderful dream about him. Leo's favourite place to be was at the cottage, where family and friends would congregate; there was always a crowd at the cottage and Leo was always the first one to greet you.

I dreamed I was in the kitchen at the cottage, when my husband came rushing in to tell me, "Come outside, everyone is out there."

As I walked out, I could see Leo, sitting in a lawn chair, in his bathing suit, and sipping his favorite drink: rye and coke. He slowly turned around to face me, and held up his drink in the air. "I'm all right, Joanne!"

Needless to say, I was overjoyed, and promptly told everyone not to worry, he's fine!

Now, I don't know if it was my brain trying to heal me, or if it was really Leo. I'd like to think it was a little bit of both.

Two Interesting Stories

Sonya Erick

I received not one but two interesting stories on June 7, 2009. They arrived by email from Sonya Erick, a first-time correspondent. I am reproducing the texts here the way they arrived, with minimal copyediting. They make great reading!

The stories are smoothly written and record the results of sessions spent with Ouija boards and also with a ghost or a poltergeist in Ms. Erick's parents' bungalow. At the end of the second story, she wonders whether her "familiar spirit" will travel with her from Regina to Toronto. I wonder, too. Perhaps she will keep us informed!

At one time, Ouija boards were more popular than they are these days, though they are still offered for sale in novelty and game stores as well as metaphysical and occult supply shops. These varnished boards, decorated with words and numbers, accompanied by their tripod-like devices called planchettes, go back to the "witch-boards" used by fortune tellers and spiritualists in the middle of the nineteenth century in the United States. Indeed, the invention of the board has often been attributed — erroneously — to Daniel Fox, brother of the infamous Fox Sisters, who in 1848 conducted the world's first seances in Hydesville, near Rochester, New York. Interestingly, Daniel and his three sisters (Katie, Maggie, and Leah) were not really Americans but early Canadians, having been born across Lake Ontario in Consecon, Ontario. Katie and Maggie are credited with being the world's first spiritualists, and Leah is credited with being their first manager.

I suggest that Ms. Erick is a "sensitive," that is, a person who is particularly responsive to sensations, emotions, thoughts, and intuitions. This is a not-uncommon condition; it is one suitable for a musician, especially a singer. Perhaps in an earlier age, Ms. Erick would have been a spirit-medium and a spiritualist like Maggie Fox! As well, it is widely believed that places are haunted. But another belief is that it is people who are haunted. Certainly, there are travelling spirits, or people who are susceptible to them. Yet, at the same time, the experiences that she describes are associated with poltergeists — disturbances rather than entity appearances. So the jury is out on what is happening.

In the meantime, here is Ms. Erick.

Dear Mr. Colombo:

I have just finished reading your book, *The Big Book of Canadian Ghost Stories*. I felt compelled to write to you about something that happened to me twelve years ago while I was a university student, and also about some recent happenings that I've encountered. I hope you will find both stories of interest. I currently reside in Regina, Saskatchewan, but will be relocating to Toronto in the next few weeks (despite the recession!). My first story takes place both in Saskatchewan and Ontario.

ONE

When I was twenty-one, I was attending the University of Regina as a music student. My major was voice. This would have been around 1994–95. At the time, the music, visual art, and drama departments were located at the College Avenue campus. This has since changed, and now the Conservatory of Music has completely taken over where there used to be classes for music majors.

Next door to that building is Darke Hall, which is known to be haunted by Frank Darke, a politician who built the hall for musical and acting performances. He is said to still haunt the hall. The conservatory building is said to be haunted by a spirit of a little girl. My boyfriend at the time was a political science major, and I had become close with his group of friends, and he with some of mine. He had a male friend who I became good friends with who was a visual arts major. The building that the visual artist and drama majors used was next to the conservatory building. These buildings were incredibly old, and he and other artists could easily break into the building late at night by just simply sliding a credit card along the bolt lock. They would go in and work on their art work at all hours.

He said one night he had seen a large, bright orb fly by him in the studio he was working in. It scared him badly, and it got us all to talking about the different ghosts that were said to haunt the College Avenue campus. Me, my boyfriend, and a female friend of his decided to do a Ouija board session. The first time, nothing happened, but the second time, we got the reaction we had been looking for.

At first we ended up speaking to a spirit of a woman who called herself Silva. She was extremely mischievous and liked to joke around with us. Then, we asked Silva to leave the board, and I asked to speak to the spirit of the little girl that was said to haunt the Conservatory Building. The way the planchette was moving instantly changed. You could feel that someone different was in the room and on the board. She claimed that she had been orphaned and was very lonely and was looking for her family. My boyfriend and I continued to speak to her every few days for a few weeks. Soon, our relationship began to change, we broke up and maintained a friendship for a while. But we were both really young, and we pretty much drifted apart due to many reasons. I decided I wanted to leave Regina as my relationship with my voice teacher had disintegrated. I felt it wasn't a good learning environment for me any longer, and I also wanted a change of scenery.

That fall, I moved to Windsor, Ontario, and finished my music degree at the University of Windsor. I had originally wanted to transfer to the University of Toronto, but I had done this on the fly at the last minute and didn't get my application in soon enough to the U of T. It probably was supposed to be that way, because I ended up meeting someone who shared my enthusiasm for the supernatural in Windsor.

One of my roommates in my dorm was a channel. She agreed to do a Ouija session with me. I was looking to have a very intense supernatural experience ... and boy did I get what I asked for. A friend of ours who lived down the hall was a skeptic, but wanted to see our session. I told him he could be a witness to it, but not come on the board, as I felt his energy was too negative for the board. He agreed. Soon after my roommate and I opened the board, my roommate asked me whom I wanted to speak with. I asked to speak to Silva, who quickly made her presence known.

In her typical mischievous way, she began to poke and tickle my roommate. Then I asked to speak with the young girl that my ex-boyfriend and I had been speaking with a year previous. We exchanged some conversation through the board, when her spirit overtook my roommate's body. She began to cry, but not the cry of a woman in her early 20s; it was a little girl's cry. The room became extremely cold.

I tried to communicate with the child and comfort her, and I took her by the hands, but she did not speak to me and continued to cry. Our other roommate came into the apartment, which scared the spirit off. My roommate's head immediately dropped and she stopped crying, the temperature in the room returned to normal. She then raised her head and asked what had happened and claimed she couldn't remember a thing. Needless to say, it scared the living "you know what" out of our skeptic friend, and I haven't taken part in a Ouija session since!

Two

I am currently living in my parent's house. I moved back in with them after living and working overseas for a couple of years. About a year ago, I woke to see a man, who I did not instantly recognize, sitting beside my bed; however, there is no chair there.

He was dressed in an old-fashioned-looking suit and was looking at me very intently with a very worried look on his face. Soon after I adjusted my eyes, to make sure I was really seeing him, he disappeared. I tried not to dwell on it, and chalked it up to a dream or being halfway between a dream and waking state.

The following day, my grandmother ended up in the hospital. Two nights later, I woke up to a man clearing his throat and some low talking in my bedroom. I didn't see him or anyone else, but I spent the next ten minutes hiding beneath my covers like a little kid.

A few days later, my sister was over at the house. I mentioned to her and my mom what had happened, and I described the way the man that had been sitting by my bed had looked. I asked my mother if any male in our family had been tall and thin with a long face and beard. My sister immediately said it was our great grandfather, my mom's grandfather. I saw a picture of him, and the man sitting beside my bed looked very much like the man in the picture.

Considerable time went by before I saw him again. He appeared to me, standing beside my bed just this past winter, but said nothing. I began noticing that at times the lights flicker in the house, but only when I am home alone, or in a room alone, never when someone else is around.

This past Easter, things kind of intensified. Sometimes the radio would be on when I know I had just turned it off, and I was home alone. But the most interesting night I had was shortly after Easter. My parents were downstairs, and I was alone upstairs. (The house is a bungalow.) There are three canisters that sit against the wall under the built-in microwave stand. I turned around to find one of the canisters that contained mini-chocolate eggs left over from Easter pushed away from the wall. I pushed it back. I turned my back for some water, but turned around to find it was moved away from the wall. I, again, pushed it back, turned my back, and heard it come away from the wall again. I guess he likes chocolate!

I got my drink and went into the dining room to get to the living room to watch TV. I had the dimmer on the dining-room chandelier set to exactly where I like it. It had been pushed all the way up as far as it could go. Bright light illuminated the room. My parents had not come upstairs, and even if they had, neither would bring the lights up that brightly. I lay down on the couch with my legs tucked in so that the last cushion on the sofa remained free. I felt my whole body go very cold, particularly my feet (especially my toes). I saw a bit of an indentation on the sofa cushion near my feet, as if someone was sitting there. I guess he likes TV too!

A couple of weeks ago, I was home alone, and was downstairs listening to music and reading, when I heard light footsteps above me. I called out — no answer. I then heard the distinct sound of a drawer in my parent's room open and close loudly and abruptly. When I went to investigate to see if either of my parents were home, I found the house empty. I wonder if he will follow me to Toronto.

Hope you enjoyed the stories!

STRANGE GOINGS-ON

Ziba Fisher

In the early 1950s, Ziba Fisher and I were members of a circle of students at Waterloo College, now Wilfred Laurier University, next to today's University of Waterloo with all its computer and engineering programs. In those days, Waterloo College was a small liberal arts college and seminary for students intent on entering the Lutheran ministry. Perhaps I should not speak for Ziba, but I will speak for myself when I say that, at the time, we were on the liberal arts side of things, not the ministry side! Members of the group drifted apart. Thereafter, Ziba and I lost contact.

Segue to March 2011. Out of the blue, I received an email from Ziba, who had checked my website and thought that we should reconnect. I am certainly pleased that he felt this way, as so did I! An exchange of emails established the fact that he had gone into business and then used his management skills to work on the campus of a community college in Toronto. He described the services he provided as those of an "independent education management professional."

From my website, he gathered that I was still concerned with the paranormal, and he asked if I would like to read an account of some of his and his wife Jean's odd experiences. When I assured him of my interest, he sent me this informal record of a number of those experiences.

Readers of this book who are only interested in haunted houses and mysterious disappearances will find the following account of Ziba's to be low-key. Indeed, what I admire about his account is precisely this quality!

How can one write about experiences that defy rational explanation?

Valid as this comment may be, I will set about to try.

A little about our circumstances — Jean and I are a retired couple, in our late 70s, happily married for decades, comfortable with ourselves and with our lives. We're not particularly religious, although each of us in our younger years believed ourselves to be Christians.

Normally, our personal concerns, thoughts, and experiences are shared with one another, and we are comfortable in so doing. Any hesitation to do so is usually because we feel it might upset the other.

But Jean overcame such a hesitation today, and I write to tell you about it.

It all began with the purchase of an attractive suitcase. Jean has never owned two cases that matched, so we decided to buy a matching set — one larger and one smaller.

There was a small hitch — the shop was short on inventory — no matching, smaller-sized case was on hand. But a solution was soon worked out. The same chain had a shop that was on our way home, and it had the desired matching case. The shops had a chain-wide promotion sale: buy one at full price, and any second case could be had for half-price. Would the shop that had the case we wanted honour the promotion price?

Of course. Simply bring along your sales slip, pretend to "return" the larger case, then re-buy it on paper, and its smaller companion is yours, at half price.

Deal!

The parting advice from the original seller: "Be sure to keep your sales slip — and make a copy of it too. The other store will need the original, and you will need your copy for guarantee purposes ..."

Arrangements firmly in place, we returned home.

But there I came to realize that the critical sales slip was missing! It just could not be found.

As may be the case with others of a certain age, I have little habits that help me remember where to look for stuff. Once such is usage of one particular portion of a well-worn wallet to store away sales slips. We get so many.... But when checked, the sales slip just wasn't there.

Then began the checking of alternatives, hopefully with good results. Pockets in trousers, shirt, outer jacket. Not there.

Re-check the wallet — any and all possible locations. To no avail.

Sheepishly, I had to admit that it looked like I might have to pay full price again, because I seemed to have mislaid the sales slip.

Jean knows from our many years of searching for passports, ownership-papers, doctor's referrals, or such, that I do not always find things that have gone astray. Things that turn out to be quite findable. She knows, because she is the one who finds them.

So, with all due deference, she suggested that it might be a good idea for us to re-check the wallet. Together, this time.

And so we did. A very thorough check it was, too. Found some things that had lost all meaning, and a few sales slips that had faded with the passage of time. But not *the* sales slip. Just was not to be found.

I was feeling badly. I knew that the sales slip was important, but I just could not account for its whereabouts.

And so to bed.

The next morning, I followed a household routine. After putting the coffee on, I came to the office to check the emails and such. Soon after, Jean joined me. I could see from her look that this was to be no ordinary morning. She looked plainly uncomfortable.

Her explanation soon followed.... She had been awake during the night and was a little concerned over my disappointment concerning the loss of the sales slip. So she acted on a hunch and re-examined my wallet.

Much to her puzzled astonishment, the sales slip was there, in very plain view, in the very same wallet we had each examined, and then had examined together. It was folded in such a manner that the name of the retail chain was plainly visible.

How is it possible that two capable people can examine, in each other's company, a well-used wallet, and not see so much as a trace of a several-times-folded white paper that now was in very, very plain view?

It certainly is a puzzle.

Were this the only occasion that questions like this were asked of one another, it might be unremarkable. But of course it isn't. We have had other "strange-goings-on" over the years.

For example, there is the case of the missing wristwatch.

Jean's wristwatch was missing. We looked high and low for it but did not find it. We continued our search, off and on, for several weeks, before coming to accept that it was not going to turn up.

A winter passed before we next took our trailer away for a weekend. On opening it, there, in plain sight, in the center of our bed, was Jean's watch. We had not yet been into our trailer for an entire season. But there was the watch.

Other quirks of experience have caused us each to arrive at very similar conclusions: we have a guest, a whimsical, sometimes irritating, always puzzling, guest.

The question: who, or what, is with us? We feel no dread, no sense of impending danger. We have not seen articles move of their own accord, nor have we heard strange sounds, or experienced any of the things we could recognize as "signs," in some traditional sense.

And there is yet another question: why?

Why is it that we are experiencing such events? Jean has whimsically suggested that the spirit of her late sister may be paying us a visit, and who is to say not? But the events have taken place, and, we rather expect, will continue to.

The account does not end at this point. It continues with an email that I received from Ziba on March 14, 2011, the day following my receipt of above text. Here it is in its entirety.

A strange thing happened the night I wrote you that note. It may be of interest too. It was about a missing earring.

Jean loves earrings. And she is most careful with them. Of course, we have stories of "lost" earrings that were recovered — unusual experiences, but entirely reasonable. But this postscript we don't think fits that description.

A favoured earring of Jean's went missing. She asked me to keep an eye open for it. She made mention of it to a nice lady who helps with the household cleaning from time to time. Just in case....

But it didn't show up.

Daughter Jackie was visiting and was also told. And she thought her eyes might be a little sharper, and together with Jean she went on yet another hunt. But to no avail.

I must make mention of the fact that both Jean and Jackie have a strong track record of finding things. They find things when no one else can. They are really good at finding.

Fast forward to the day after I wrote my letter to you. I am once again at the computer, when Jean brings tea and an announcement: "It's happened again." You can guess....

Indeed, there, in plain sight, on her bedside table, right where one would first look for it, was the missing earring.

Coincidence? I think not.

I Just Want to Tell Someone

Eileen Foley

This one-paragraph text arrived by email early Friday night, May 8, 2009, under a subject line that asked a question: "Are you still collecting stories?" I read it with deep fascination. The account has a dynamism of its own, and I was dazzled by the writer's willingness to share her emotions and experiences with me and our future readers. I added a little bit of punctuation here and there and sent the text back to the woman, asking her for a name and as much biographical information as she wished to share. Her reply, received the next day, appears at the end of the account. The two accounts make interesting reading, so I am grateful for Mrs. Foley for preserving these memories.

ACCOUNT ONE

I don't know if you will find this of interest or not, or if it is a "ghost story" or a "love story," but I just want to tell someone. I met the man I would marry on Christmas Eve, 1949. A week later, he asked me to wear his ring. I said we hardly knew each other. He said we had known each other all our lives. He was right! We were married that following June, and spent almost forty-seven years together. We have a son and seven daughters, and a wonderful daughter-in-law, sons-in-law, grandchildren and great-grandchildren. When he was dying, and he well knew he was, my husband told me he wouldn't be around anymore to look after me, and I must rely on St. Joseph. I thought, "Yeah, right."

On the date of our wedding anniversary, I just wanted to get away out of town, away from anyone who might call me. So, after early morning Mass, I went for a drive. My husband's hometown was a little Ottawa Valley village called Douglas, and he rests there, in St. Michael's churchyard, with his ancestors and relatives. I went to his grave that morning, fully intending to go on to Renfrew to see the new Walmart, which had just opened. I sat beside his grave for a bit, said the Rosary, bade him goodbye, and got in the car to go to Renfrew. However, at the gate, the car turned right instead of left. Not what I wanted, at all. I got to Kelly's Corner, put on my right blinker, and the car turned left. "Okay, if this is what you want, but you drive. I don't like this road, and I have no idea where we are going." The car, with little effort on my part, took me through Eganville to Combermere, and the Madonna House gift shop. "Well," thought I, "this is really weird."

In the gift shop, I asked if they might have a St. Joseph statue. The lady said, "Not likely," as they sold quickly, but if there was one it would be in such a place. Sure enough, there he was! A little the worse for wear, his paint worn, just what my husband would have chosen! What could I do! St. Joseph came home with me. No matter what my problems, I just have to say, "St. Joseph, please help me!" and he does. One of my grandsons has that statue now, and I don't know if he regards it as anything more than something on his dresser or not.

I often get the feeling of a very heavy hand on my left shoulder, and I get such a chill (even on the hottest day) that I shiver. I'm convinced it's the love of my life, keeping tabs on me, making sure all is well. He comes to me frequently in dreams, checking up on the family. He tells me when someone is in trouble (I dream about them) and lets me know when all is well. Frankly, I can't wait to get to the other side, to continue our life together, because that is what it is, a life. Thank you for letting me get this off my mind! I will supply my name and address if you are interested. Thanks.

ACCOUNT TWO

My name is Eileen Foley. My husband and I met at a Christmas Eve party at his cousin's house in Pembroke. We were married in

Pembroke and lived the first few months of our married life there, moving to an area known locally as Pine Valley, before my husband eventually became the postmaster in Douglas, where we lived for some years, until a fire destroyed our house, when we then moved to Pembroke. We lived there until my husband died.

I should finish the tale by telling you that when I left Madonna House I got on a road I did not know and really had no idea where I was. It was one of those lovely rambling back roads, and I just kept on until it came to a spot I knew, and then I went to Renfrew, determined to see the new Walmart! Now, I always received roses for our anniversary — sometimes it was a bag of Five Roses flour, or a picture (times were not always financially great) but always, roses. That day I arrived at the parking lot, found my way, not into Walmart, but the main mall entrance, and found a group selling roses for some charity. I bought a bunch, went to the car, and just sat there until I recovered my senses. Then I went home, the visit to the new store forgotten!

I Have a Strange Ability

Andrea Fraser

I received this unusual email on July 17, 2009, and read it with a sense of excitement. It is written in the stream-of-consciousness style, jumping from thought to thought, and so there is very little introspection. But it is an honest account of how one person sees her "strange ability" and how it has affected her life.

That person is Andrea Fraser of Kamloops, B.C., and the strange ability that she describes is what Charles Fort, an American author of books that collect peculiarities and oddities from the world's press, would call a "wild talent." Ms. Fraser's wild talent seems to be in the field of *psi* — psychical powers like clairvoyance and clairaudience — and one of these is premonition. Apparently, she can see into the future. There is a grand argument as to whether such an ability exists, and if it does, whether it is merely a refinement of a natural talent or some super-added paranormal power — she may be an exceptionally acute observer of other people, or she may have access to some inner cache of supernatural power.

I do not have the answers to questions like these, and I expect that Ms. Fraser lacks them as well. But psychologists are ever on the lookout for people who profess such supernatural abilities and have been known to characterize them as "fantasy-prone personalities." Yet fantasies are part of everyday life and thought, and are often a good guide to reasonable action in an unreasonable world; just ask Carl Jung.

I Have a Strange Ability

Dear Mr. Colombo,

Hi, my name is Andrea and I live in Kamloops, B.C., Canada. I love your books. I have had several experiences in my life that are unexplainable, but interesting and never frightening to me or my family. I never had the opportunity to meet my parents' parents, as all four were deceased before my birth, and my mother has a strong feeling I am both of my grandmothers come back. I was born a sickly baby and wasn't expected be alive at two weeks old. My parents were told to take me home and make me comfortable. I surprised the doctors! I am 30 years old now. I had learning difficulties as a kid and had no friends. I was picked on in school, so I didn't talk a lot as a kid. I spent a lot of time with dolls as my friends, but forced myself to give that up at just before my 13th birthday. Maybe this had some effects on me. I have always been called the weird one in my family. I've said things and have caused fights, because I haven't known enough to pick and choose when to speak or what to say, but I've done a lot better as I've gotten older. I seem to drive people crazy with my obsession with the paranormal and dreams and reincarnation and ghosts and psychics.

I've been raised as a mainline Protestant, Trinity-accepting Christian my whole life, being taken to church at twelve days old and baptized in the Anglican faith, and I was sent to a Catholic elementary school for seven years. I adopted Lutheranism six years ago as my choice of belief for the rest of the time I get to have on Earth.

I am a dreamer and have had them come true. I used to have the gift of knowing conception in women and knowing the gender of the baby, and around age five, sometimes as a "game," my parents would ask me if somebody we knew was going to get a baby and what is it going to be. I'd say yes or no, and if it was yes, I'd say, "Yes!" "Suzy is getting a baby and she is getting a girl baby." That was fine and dandy and my parents would laugh and say, "So Suzy is getting baby and she is getting a girl baby is she?" I'd then say, "Uh-huh." So time would go by, but Suzy wasn't announcing or showing she was pregnant, but not a whole lot of time later, the word of mouth would travel around and lo and behold, "Did you hear Suzy just found she is pregnant?" My parents were never surprised, and of course, several months later, Suzy brings home a girl baby.

I've for some reason grown out of this talent, but it creeps up on me the odd time and surprises me I can still do it. As I've become older, I've noticed personally I have a strange ability to look at a child on the bus or somewhere, and their first name will suddenly jump into my brain by way of a sudden image of a person I know with that name. It doesn't happen all the time. It took a few times to sink in this was something supernatural that was going on. The first time is always a possibly coincidence, but a second and a third time is astronomical in ability.

I am constantly receptive to one talent I have: suddenly a name and a face will jump into my head, and I'm forced to think about them and how they must be doing, and I haven't seen them for a few months, and if I'm in a grocery store, about 98% of the time, the person I just began thinking about and myself nearly bump carts, as we exit the two aisles in the grocery store, or if I'm walking down a street and it comes over me, sure enough they are coming down the street toward me or coming around a corner, or if I'm at a bus stop, the bus arrives and they are sitting on it. We have call display on our phone, but I don't need it. Ninety percent of phone calls that ring in I can say the name and my husband will ask me how I knew that would be so and so. "I just knew," I tell him.

I don't know if this next one is supernatural or not, but I'll be somewhere, even out of town, and somebody will come up to me and just ask me how my parents are doing. I cautiously answer that they are fine, being a bit nervous of a "stranger," and all the time the person will say, "You are Bill and Sandra Benz's daughter, aren't you?" I'll be taken by surprise and tell them, "Yeah." I'll be like "How do you know?" I'm thinking in my head this can't be possible because I don't live here and I've never seen this person in my life, but sure enough, the person will say something like, "I used to live in Kamloops years ago and I knew your Dad or I knew your Mom. You look just like them." They'll tell me to say hi to my parents when I see them again.

I'll also have the opposite effect, where I become friends with somebody and upon sharing them with my parents, the person and my parents knew each other years ago or have family members who knew each other and suddenly I'm remembered by the person as being that cute tiny blond thing in the diaper. I have had dark hair since the age of seven. This had a positive effect on me once, where my husband was in the psychiatric ward for some treatment, and I was nervous and was trying to be a responsible adult and not get judged as being "something," considering the place my husband was at and all. It was hard, but the doctors and the nurses never did say a word and one day my dad comes to visit and one nurse was all over my dad, saying "Hi," because my Dad worked for many years at the hospital, and she was asking him what brings him to this place today and he told her he was coming to visit his son-in-law. There was a questioning face, "Son-in-law? Which patient would he be now?" Just calm and naturally, like it is no big deal because it isn't in our family, my Dad simply says, "Keith Fraser." There was a light up of excitement and almost hyperness, and she was like, "Keith? Keith? You are Keith's father-in-law?" and in seconds she looks right at my face and has a grin and calls me by my childhood nickname. "Annie! That's you? You're her?" I nodded. She then said, "I knew you and your brother when you were a tiny blond thing. You were fun little kids." My husband's psychiatrist was not as vocally excited, but kinda smiled, because he then recognized me from years ago, and the funny thing was, we were treated almost like VIPs for the remainder of the treatment in hospital, which was only about a week, and Keith came home just fine.

I had an experience where I allowed two gentleman to sit in the two extra chairs that were at a table my husband and I were sitting at because the place was crowded, and I had previously met the one gentleman and had sometimes talked at the bus stop the odd time or just waved, walking down the street, but hadn't for a couple years now, but anyway, I allowed them to sit and have their lunch in the restaurant at our table. My husband was nervous and had to be prompted to speak up, and I was being friendly and not trying to look stupid so they wouldn't think I'm weird or something, and then after fifteen minutes, I guess it was, the man simply says to me, "How are your mom and dad doing?" I responded the way I do, and said they were doing fine. The man said, "You are Bill the grocery man's daughter! I know your Mom and Dad very well." The man has since joined a group I was already in, and we talk a lot more now and are friends. He is very nice!

Other experiences I have are if I'm walking down a street and I can see someone is still quite a ways down, I'll get the overpowering sensation to cross the road and not walk past that person for any reason, or even if it is stranger, sometimes, I'll be instantly drawn to say "Hi" to that person. It makes no sense to me. I just seem to know in my gut who to be near and not be near. My husband doesn't get these feeling unless it is like once in a blue moon or something, whereas with me it is ever-present. I constantly yank my husband from walking into the path of an oncoming car that suddenly comes out of nowhere, and he will ask me how I could have possibly known that it was coming, because he didn't hear or see anything. I tell him, "I felt it." The funny thing is, I don't drive because I am too chicken to learn. Nowadays I say I don't want to learn on purpose.

I'll have experiences where I'll rent videos I want to see and I'll spend my time searching and selecting the best ones, and sure enough I always seem to select a video for the week that within two or three days suddenly is chosen for the movie of the week on a channel on TV. It's becoming a joke.

I am almost done, but I have one more to share today and it happened just recently on June the 9th, 2009. I had the weirdest dream, where an elderly woman kept reappearing in several dreams throughout the night and kept saying she needed to get a hold of my mother she had known her many years ago. I told my mom and she thought that was interesting, but a few weeks went by and nothing happened, and then suddenly just last week, my mom got a phone call out of the blue and was asked if her name was Sandra and my mom said yes and the lady asked if she was George Strange's daughter and my mom said yes and she wanted to know who this was calling her. It turned out to be my mom's second cousin, and she had been trying to find my Mom. She wanted to a hold of her, and finally she found my mom on the Internet, and so my mom and her cousin got in to talking and my mom brought up the dream her daughter had had very recently. The lady said to my mom it is funny she would say that, because she had had a dream in June and it was identical, except the old lady didn't speak in her dream. I never knew this lady existed and she had her dream in Massachusetts, United States, and I had my dream in Kamloops, British Columbia, Canada.

Street Lamp Interference

David Gallinger

I am a long-time subscriber to *The Skeptical Inquirer*, the journal for critical inquiry that was founded in 1976 in Buffalo, New York. It was published bimonthly by the Committee for the Scientific Investigation of Claims of the Paranormal, a group that shortened its name to Center for Inquiry. Originally, its remit was limited to "claims of the paranormal," excluding those of belief systems. By this the editors meant it would study reports of anomalous phenomena, like the basis for *The Amityville Horror*, sightings of ghosts and flying saucers, accounts of mind reading, claims of cancer cures, and other such oddities. The editors steered clear of organized religion, although there were short news stories about such matters as miraculous visions and miracle cures, and there was always an article or two to debunk believers' claims for the antiquity of the Shroud of Turin. In the last decade or so, the editors have put their boxing gloves on and begun to do battle with militant religionists. They have commissioned major examinations of so-called Scientific Creationism, Intelligent Design, the Gaia Hypothesis, Global Warming, the encroachments of religious fundamentalists on individual rights and freedom of expression, and similar subjects.

The journal's letters to the editor column is always stimulating to read, never more so than when it published the following letter in the May–June 2009 issue. It was contributed by David Gallinger of Edmonton, Alberta, who wrote about what has been called "street lamp interference." This is a phenomenon well-described in *Skeptical Inquirer*'s article

"The Curious Case of Street Lamp Interference" (January–February 2009), which elicited Mr. Gallinger's reply. I associate the phenomenon with the investigations and analyses of Hilary Evans, a well-respected English author who wrote about anomalous phenomena and devoted a book-length study to the oddity. What I find particularly interesting about street lamp interference is that it seems related to a phenomenon noted in the Arctic by the Inuit and explorers: snapping one's fingers can make stars blink out!

I have Mr. Gallinger's permission to reproduce a slightly revised version of his letter. When I queried him about his background, he wrote, on May 12, 2009, "My bio is rather short because there's nothing really notable to say about me. Here it is: David is a musician and writer based in Edmonton, Alberta. He no longer believes in ghosts although he has met some rather charming ones in the past."

Recently, I read an article in the *Skeptical Inquirer* about a paranormal experience called "Street Lamp Interference." I was amused to read their speculation about the possible cause of these hauntings. The theories were just as complex and over-thought as anything I would expect from a scientist, and they all amounted to the simplistic assumption that the haunted people are crazy. I myself encountered this mystery in my teenage years, and despite being a 14-year-old boy of no notable intelligence, I was able to harness that metaphysical phenomenon for the one purpose that singularly drove my existence at that age: *schadenfreude*. And also, impressing pretty girls.

The victim of this strange demonic oppression was a girl my age, named Amanda, who lived on the other half of my parents' duplex. She was terribly superstitious. Normally, I would have rushed to debunk such a person's beliefs and made a quick enemy, but in her case, well, I had a good reason to indulge her. She was pretty.

She was pretty, but gullible. She believed that her brother had brought demons into the house by listening to heavy metal and insisted that she was cursed. She saw every trivial event as evidence that evil spirits were following her around, and I set about trying to prove her wrong. In my own mind, I was not trying to debunk her beliefs but rather to free her from her fear of these coincidences.

She believed that a particular streetlight on our block was possessed and would harass her by shutting off whenever she passed it. She said it "almost always" happened. This was her ultimate evidence that the curse was real; the light's behaviour was a harbinger of death. So I set about to disprove this. To my relief, she was unable to replicate the circumstances. She walked past the light numerous times and it did nothing. I told her that these lamps turn on and off when they burn out and that with the light flickering constantly, it was inevitable that there would be an occasional correlation if she passed it daily. She accepted this logic, and she felt very relieved.

Unfortunately, a short time later the light resumed its assault on her sanity.

I'd gone out with a few of my friends at around seven in the evening. It was early in the fall and since our city is far to the north, it was already getting quite dark. We went to her house to meet up with her, and as we were leaving, the light shut off. She *screamed*. I was determined to prove that it was a fluke. So I set up a controlled experiment that involved each of us walking past the light in a random order while taking care to pass it at exactly the same point. To my shock, she was right!

Every time she walked past it, the light would shut off. But it didn't happen to anyone else. She was very upset; her faith in my skepticism was lost. She thought she was going to die. We decided the best way to quell her teenage histrionics was to simply get her the hell away from that damned light. She calmed down a bit, but on the way back home, she refused to pass it again. She was terrified and wouldn't budge. She insisted that she would stay outside all night, no matter how cold it got.

As we struggled in vain to assuage her fears, another girl in the group decided that she was fed up and had decided to go on home without us. It was too cold to stand around in the dark and argue. In fact, she'd been complaining all evening that it was cold. Amanda had lent her jacket to that girl, to persuade her to stay with us so that she wouldn't end up being the only female in the group. But as the other girl stormed off she suddenly stopped in her tracks when *the light shut off!*

She came darting back and the light turned on. She returned and it shut off. Now she was the one freaking out. She accused my neighbour of passing on the curse to her. While storming off, she was reminded that she still had her friend's jacket and reacted by throwing it on the ground. I went to pick up the jacket and retrieve it. As soon as I picked it up, the light shut off again. Then I screamed.

I ran back to the group and one of the other guys jokingly suggested that it was the jacket that was haunted. Well, Amanda felt that made perfect sense. She decided to burn it. I stopped her, but not in the interests of rescuing that hideous and gaudy example of early 1990s fashion; I wanted to experiment further. I put on the jacket and tried walking backwards and forwards, walking at different speeds, and wearing the jacket inside out. This was the breakthrough. The jacket was a bright neon yellow, but the lining was dark blue. We set about examining all the lights nearby to see if there was anything different about this one. We discovered that the evil light had a small black dot on it, toward the back of the fixture. I held up the jacket toward that dot and the light shut off. We replicated it with a mirror as well and it worked more reliably. The light would shut off for 30 seconds, then turn on and rapidly shut off again if the mirror was still in place. My friend's anxiety ebbed as the ghost that haunted her now vanished in a puff of logic. I felt like a hero.

On another night I got together with the guys and we gathered as many flashlights as we could find. We pointed them at the dot just to see what would happen. This time instead of turning on again after 30 seconds, it stayed off. At the 30 second mark all the nearby lights also shut off.

We determined that the little dot was a photocell that turned the light on at dusk and off at dawn. Since the cell was pointed down and was so close to a light source, it was prone to interference from reflections. To rule this out, it was programmed to shut off just the one light and wait. If the light level stayed high it would shut off the other lights, and if not, it would turn back on. We found other lights that were similarly equipped and discovered that we could turn them off simply by shining one flashlight from behind a fence. This made it possible to convince people that we could shut them off *with the power of our minds.*

Regrettably, I can no longer replicate the circumstances of this anecdote. All the street lights in Edmonton were replaced a few years ago because the old ones have rusted and toppled over. The city wasn't careful enough about checking the credentials of the company that installed them, and ended up paying a premium price for a very cheap alloy. The new lights have a different control system, which is much more difficult to hack.

I would suggest that this particular phenomenon might be best explained by questioning the local boys about their familiarity with the lights' control system; once I figured out how it worked, I must admit that I caused a few other people to think they were possessed.

THIRD MAN FACTOR

John Geiger

John Geiger is an enthusiast for explorations of two worlds — of the inner world of the spirit and of the outer world of nature. As such, he is a travel writer of liminal or borderline states, and in this regard rather resembles two other anthropologists with Canadian backgrounds: Wade Davis from the West Coast, who was attracted to the zombies of Haiti, and Edmund Carpenter, who taught anthropology at the University of Toronto and roamed the Arctic and much of the rest of the world, making notes in the process.

Born in Ithaca, based in Toronto, Geiger has written a number of unusual books of uncommon interest. Here are the titles of his first four books: *Nothing Is True* (a study of the postmodernist Brion Gysin), *Frozen in Time* (a record of a photographic expedition to the Far North), *Dead Silences* (an account of Arctic exploration), and *The Third Man Factor* (an examination of "the sense of presence").

With Geiger's permission, I am able to reproduce here the following account of the last work, consisting of questions and his answers, in his own words, because it is germane to the subject of the present book.

WHAT IS THE THIRD MAN FACTOR?

Many people who have survived life and death struggles have come forward to describe encounters with an incorporeal being who provided them with companionship, encouragement, guidance and hope, helping them to live. A good number of these cases involve people in extreme and unusual environments, such as the polar regions, alone at sea, or when climbing at high altitudes. However, other people, when confronted with personal stress under certain conditions, also encounter an unseen presence. In this book I have gathered together a large number of Third Man reports. I spoke to scores of people to try to understand what conditions are necessary to provoke the experience, how it affected them, and what explanations exist for the Third Man Factor. The book is my attempt to answer one question: "What is going on here?" Where does the name "Third Man" come from?

The explorer Sir Ernest Shackleton had the experience in 1916 during his legendary escape from Antarctica after his ship *Endurance* was trapped and then crushed by the ice. Shackleton and two of his men were on the final leg of their harrowing journey. They had to cross an uncharted mountain range on the British possession of South Georgia, a sub-Antarctic island, in order to reach help at a whaling station. During that mountainous crossing each one of the three men had the sense that there was another "presence" with them, helping them. This became known as the fourth presence. But it didn't end there. The Anglo-American poet T.S. Eliot was inspired by Shackleton's story of an unseen companion, and included it in *The Waste Land*, the most famous poem of the 20th century. But Eliot changed the number, writing: "Who is the third who walks always beside you?" Because of this, the experience became known among climbers and other explorers as the "third man factor" or sometimes "third man syndrome."

WHY DID YOU WRITE THE THIRD MAN FACTOR?

When I was a child I had a very interesting experience. I was hiking with my father, a geologist, in southern Alberta, when I was confronted by a rattlesnake. My father was ahead of me, so it was a pretty terrifying encounter. Except that I had a sense that I was immediately detached from the scene. I viewed what unfolded from another, impossible angle. It was as if I were separated from my physical body. I always thought the whole thing very strange, and later put it down to a child's over-active imagination. Then, when reading Shackleton's book *South*, I realized that other people also had strange experiences when under extreme stress. I began searching, and immediately came across other examples, much like Shackleton's. Like Frank Smythe's meeting with an unseen companion high on Mount Everest, and Charles Lindbergh's experience during his Atlantic crossing in the *Spirit of St. Louis*. I was hooked. I found many others, and then people started to bring me examples. Some involved people caught in natural and man-made disasters, including 9/11. I realized it was a very common occurrence, and began to think that people are in fact hard-wired for the Third Man. That makes the Third Man Factor not just an absolutely fascinating subject to write about, but something that can touch all of our lives in a positive way, under the right conditions.

SEVERAL OF MY EXPERIENCES

Sally Huggard

For some reason or other I did not receive this letter, which bears the date May 26, 2010, until August 23, 2010. It had been addressed to me care of my publisher, Dundurn, but the editorial department did not receive it until August 18. Sally Huggard's envelope, mailed from Winnipeg to an address in Toronto, bore the right amount of postage, but the stamp was unfranked. Odd. But then, Mrs. Huggard's letter is full of descriptions of odd and inexplicable happenings.

Not all ghost stories are about "ghosts," ethereal beings of some sort or other; most of them are about feelings, perceptions, sensations, thoughts, and happenings. Mrs. Huggard's account is full of peculiar occurrences of that sort, and I like her account because she simply records what happened to her over a number of years and then leaves it to her readers to make of these experiences what they can. At the end, she refers to the Polaroid taken by her late husband and also to regular photographs taken by their best friend. The former shows an anomalous shape like a cloud — but a cloud indoors! The other photographs show, again, cloud-like swirls. I have no idea what created them, for they could be ascribed to double-exposures, to light leakages, to development stains, or to spirits!

May 26, 2010

Dear Mr. Colombo:

Before me are two of your books recently purchased from the Doubleday Book Club. I've just begun reading *The Big Book of Canadian Ghost Stories* and felt compelled to write you about several of my experiences. At this writing it is three years this month my husband, Robert John, has died — a coincidence that your name is reversed. He died at home after a four-day illness.

During those days, I kept up the early morning feeding of birds and squirrels near the garage. This was something he had done faithfully, so I am still doing it — however, on the day or rather the early morning he died, I noticed a few black leaves on the sidewalk, which was unusual for May and generally if they had been from fall, they would be brown.... I tried, oh how I tried, to sweep them off the walk, but they only whirled about. I gave up, and when my sister-in-law arrived from Thunder Bay, to spend a few days with me during this time, I took her outside to show her the leaves. Not one was in sight!

The second incident was a sudden flock of black birds. Unusual for having them in May, as generally one would see them in late summer.

After I was alone again, my neighbour helped carry in groceries through the back, and when she left, I began putting them away, but glanced towards the screen door to see a dozen or more black flies. Puzzled, I shooed them outdoors, then closed the inner door, but the house was warm, so I opened that door to find the exact number of flies inside again. Now I am frightened. How did they get in both times? Again, I shooed them out and for the rest of the year never saw another fly.

Since his passing, I have had to get rid of the bed he died on. There had been knocking close to my head. I moved into the back bedroom, and just recently had one rap near my pillow. And just a week ago in August, three more.

Now I'll take you back over some other incidents in my life. I am now eighty-one, and will be eighty-two by the time this appears in your book, but I can remember many details. Having had no siblings — and during my fifty-seven years of marriage, no children. At age thirteen, I dreamt of my much-loved grandfather's boots on the steps of a funeral home. He died, aged fifty-six, near Christmas. In August of 1956, while we lived in the then Fort William, Ontario, I dreamed of a grave with one peach-coloured gladiola on it. In September my fifty-four-year-old father died. After the funeral, while Mother's home in Selkirk, Manitoba, was filled with people, I was off by myself near the front door, when something drew me outside. Mother always had a lovely flower garden, but all were frozen that week. I made my way down the walk and discovered one lone peach gladiola still intact!

My closest friend I met at fourteen had multiple sclerosis and lived in my hometown, until we lived in Ontario. She choked on a fishbone in 1967 and went into a coma. In January of 1968, I was dreaming she came to see me by my bed. All dressed up and laughing. Told me to contact three of our friends. Upon rising, my Mother phoned from Selkirk, telling me Edith had died. "I know," I said. That day was spent contacting our friends, as my dream requested.

I have had many dreams that came to pass. Generally, it could take a long time, but they do eventually happen. While living in Ontario, visiting my Mother often — once in the 70s, Robert and I parked off the road to have a sleep in the car so we wouldn't get to her too early. My head was against the open window and I found myself floating from there across the next field. I began to struggle, and saw myself looking back at me and thinking, "Oh, you're afraid," and swoosh, I was back drenched in a cold mist....

The last episode I had when staying overnight at Mother's was in 1972. I came by Greyhound bus, as Robert was working. Mother rose early, but I was still in bed when I was awakened by thoroughly being kissed, and no one was there. Frightened, I ran downstairs to tell Mother, and she said she wasn't surprised, as someone was always pulling down her blankets as she slept. She lived alone, so wasn't she frightened? I guess not. Maybe I do take after her.

The last straw to this day still baffles me. We moved into this house in 1978, 1st of May. (Many things happen in May.) Getting ready for bed in a quiet house, we heard this noise, but didn't know what made it, until next day when Robert went down to the basement. A solid hanger that holds shirts or blouses was found on the cement floor, a yard away from a clothesline. How could that happen?

Then, on a shopping day, he took ten pounds of potatoes down to the basement and set them on the table. When I went down, I thought I should move them. As I went to pick them up, my mind went completely blank. To this day I don't know where they disappeared to. And there you have it.

With a Polaroid camera, when Rob woke up to a noise in the corner of the bedroom, he took this photo I'm enclosing. If he could have held it higher, a head might have shown, as it looks like a woman seated there. I'd be interested to know what you think. To me it resembles a woman's body without her head. Hopefully you'll write me, please.

Yours sincerely,
Sally Huggard

P.S. I have no Internet. At eighty-one, I don't feel like learning. I do read a lot and thankfully I am in good health. S.

Mrs. Huggard, in a separate letter, dated August 30, 2010, wrote as follows:

Now this occurred just three days ago. Another three knocks by my pillow, waking me from a sound sleep. The next morning, I moved my bed into my dressing room.

My friend Patrick Belhumeur came with his camera just yesterday ... an orb again. It is still in his camera, so it hasn't been developed yet.

We did find out that in the early Sixties, a woman who lived here, with three children, killed herself! On this note, I will close with my sincere thanks.

P.S. My wall murals show a strange, whale-like creature.

Various Incidents

George Kocik

At least once a week, I receive an email from a reader of one of my "ghost books." The reader has taken seriously my invitation to contribute a story or two to a future book. (These books are not limited to sightings of ghosts, of course, but are collections of first-person accounts of encounters that may be described as supernatural or paranormal, psychical or clairvoyant, in nature.) I am always pleased to receive letters or emails from readers, and I try to respond to them "before the sun sets" — that is, within twenty-four hours.

George Kocik sent me three emails, which I received on January 21, 2010. I find they make interesting reading because they are straightforward, matter-of-fact, and free of the jargon of so-called ghost hunters and self-styled psychics. The experiences that Mr. Kocik describes took place in his childhood and in his mature years. I wonder if they will continue to occur to him so they may be companions throughout his life. If so, he has an interesting life! I have no explanation for what he has experienced, other than to observe that "such things be" and they occur more widely and often than they are reported, as few people are as forthright as Mr. Kocik.

That is not the end of it. My correspondent began to recall other experiences and share our mutual enthusiasm for poetry, in this instance writing it rather than reading it! So I have added these emails, which I received the next day, January 22, 2010. Readers may wish to access Mr. Kocik's poems ... whether they are the product of free association or automatic writing or poetic inspiration is another matter to be discussed on another occasion!

PAST LIVES

Hello Mr. Colombo:

I'm presently reading your book, *The Midnight Hour*. Here are two incidents that may interest you.

In 1957 I was eight years old. We didn't have a car. We lived in Val-d'Or, Quebec, at the time. One Sunday in July, my mother and I went to Ville Marie (some hundred-odd miles away) with our neighbours and their son. We had never been there before. As I walked downhill on the wooden sidewalk towards Lake Temiskaming, I got the eerie feeling that I'd walked these sidewalks before. I suddenly got the sensation of carrying a heavy backpack on my shoulders. As I stood on the dock in the sunlight, all present-day sounds ceased around me, and I had a brief flash of birchbark canoes and men in buckskins. I must add that Lake Temiskaming was a heavily used water route during the fur-trading days. It was as if I'd stepped into another time. As I said, the flash was brief, and I had to blink my eyes.

The second incident happened a couple of weeks later. Again with the same family, we had gone to Lake Tiblemont (about thirty miles from Val-d'Or) to watch the regatta. On that sunny afternoon, while everyone was watching the motor boats, I again got a flash of birchbark canoes, Indians, and white men ploughing through the waters of the lake. I also got a deep feeling of sadness about the place, as if something tragic had happened there. Although I have never been to sea, I love everything about it. Stories, pictures, memorabilia, etc.

This, and the two experiences I just related, make me believe that I lived past lives as a sailor and later as a *coureur des bois*.

Hello Mr. Colombo:

I'm writing you about an experience that may interest you. In the fall of 1977, I'd been married only a couple of months. I knew that my wife's grandfather was in an old-age home in Sarnia and that he was in poor health. I had seen pictures of him, but had never met the man. One night, I dreamt that I was alone in a funeral home with a corpse. I had no idea who was in the coffin. All I knew was that I had to wait for someone to come along to relieve me. The coffin was in the centre of the room. On the walls was grayish and purple wallpaper. The curtains and the chairs were also purple and a sort of velour material.

The funeral home stood at the corner of two streets. The driveway was an arc with an entrance and exit onto the same street. In the foreground was a stand of shrubbery and flowers. It was getting dark and I was getting anxious to be gone. I looked out the window and saw the silhouettes of three people coming: a tall woman, a short woman, and a short man. I knew it was these people I'd been waiting for and my dream ended. I told my wife about it and she told her mother.

Two days later, my wife's grandfather died. On her return from the funeral, my mother-in-law asked me if I'd ever been to Petrolia. Jokingly, I asked her in French, "*Qu'est-ce que ça mange en hiver?*" What does it eat in winter? I had never heard of Petrolia. Then she proceeded to describe the funeral home I'd seen in my dream. The tall woman was her. The short woman was her sister, and the short man her brother. Years later, at a family gathering in Oil Springs, I was shown the funeral home in Petrolia.

A Ghostly Visitor?

Hello again, Mr. Colombo:

Here is an incident that happened in 1981. We were renting an apartment in my mother's home and she lived above us. In September of that year, she passed away. Her apartment stayed unoccupied for a long time. Her bedroom was right above ours. In the deep of night, we could hear footsteps above us. It was an old house and we passed it off as the sounds that go with an old house.

One afternoon in October, I was sitting in the living room watching TV. I happened to glance out the window and saw an elderly woman in a beige trench coat coming up the sidewalk. She was the same stature as my mother had been and looked exactly like her. She had the same kind of trench coat that my mother had. The resemblance was so striking that I sprang from my chair to rush to the door so that I might see this woman as she passed by. When I opened the door, there was nobody in the street. From my seat to the door took about two seconds.

In the months that passed, strange things began to happen. Sometimes the bathroom light would go on in the middle of the night, or the bathroom door opened by itself. Sometimes the TV would go on around three in the morning. We thought perhaps our daughter had gotten up during the night, but upon inspection, she would be sound asleep.

After the apartment was rented, these things stopped. The house has been sold since. My daughter now has a three-month-old daughter of her own. She giggles and coos as she lies on her play mat. I think she sees my mother who is keeping an eye on us.

ADDITIONAL EMAILS

Hello Mr. Colombo:

I was rereading your email just now and another experience came to mind. In 1985, the mine where I worked closed. I was out of work for close to a year, so I had plenty of time to wait at my daughter's bus stop to keep a watch over her and the other kids. (I had taken it upon myself to be their guardian, because a pedophile was on the prowl and had recently attacked a young girl.) A close friend of mine owned an assay office right next to the bus stop, and every morning we'd exchange words, which would end in me reminding him to keep me in mind if he needed someone. Anyway, July came and I was still out of a job. My unemployment insurance had ended. On the day I went to apply for welfare, I got a phone call from my friend on my return home. He had a job for me. When could I start?

It was on a Friday. I started the Monday after. Through the course of time, I became close friends with another employee. (Call him Bill.) We visited, exchanged suppers, etc. The couple had four children. The youngest (she must have been about two at the time) had a heart defect since birth. Periodically, she would have to go to Montreal for treatment. The parents were in despair, for the doctors had little hope for the girl's survival.

One evening while Bill sat across from me at his table with tears in his eyes (we'd been drinking pretty heavily), he confessed his fears that his daughter wouldn't live past three or four years. I looked at him with sadness, and suddenly something like a cloud of light appeared over his head, and I said, "No. Your daughter will not die. She will grow old and you too and she will marry." That night I dreamt that I was at a wedding. The bride had long blond hair. I saw Bill and his wife sitting in the front seats. They were old and grey. Their daughter was the only child with blond hair. I told Bill and his wife about my dream the next time we got together. They said if that ever happened, they'd invite me to the wedding. The daughter consequently had a heart transplant, finished high school, and got a job with an air company. She met a young man and got married. Recently, the young couple had a baby. I lost contact with the family after I left the company. Bill and his wife forgot about their promise, but that's okay. I'm just happy that my dream came into fulfillment.

— • • • • • —

Dear Mr. Colombo:

I'm very happy that you enjoyed my accounts and that you took the time to answer me. Everything looks fine as it is. I was just about to enquire about any future publications using this material and how to acquire it.

One very odd incident I must relate to you is that in the last twenty years, I've become a very accomplished poet. I've had some poems published by poetry.com, now Lulu poetry. Over the years I've written over sixty poems. How can I explain this? Let me try. Automatic writing? Maybe. Automatic dictation? Perhaps. I don't know. In solitary moments, on the midnight shift at the mine where I used to work and later on rounds as a watchman, a voice (maybe my own inner voice) would dictate to me and I would hastily write down what I heard on any piece of paper I could find. Most recently, the voice comes in my sleep and I have to get up to write, lest I forget by morning. Like one of your readers, I also received an "editor's choice" award (two in fact). Now, the funny part about it is that I was a mediocre student in school and my worst subject was English Literature, which includes poetry. The teachers hated me and I had no love for them. I still write poetry and am presently writing a memoir of my adventures as a boy in a Northern Quebec mining town (ranging from the middle '50s to the middle '60s). My dream is to one day have my work published, but the funding is lacking.

George Kocik

Eerie Tales

Daniel Kolos

Here are two eerie tales. Like most such true tales, they are quite brief. They were written at my request by Daniel Kolos, an Egyptologist, writer, and lecturer who has a dab hand when it comes to writing about his thoughts and experiences, which he does in articles and essays and also in books of poetry. He was born in Hungary, raised in the United States, but now lives on a farm in mid-Northern Ontario. He is a friend whom I see too seldom. After knowing him for some years, he volunteered that he had two odd experiences that might well be of interest to me for my next book. He was right: they are of interest, and so here they are ... in my "next" book — an act of prophecy!

Magnetic Hill ... or Dead Soldiers?

In December 1968, I had just picked out a paperback on Nostradamus at a Philadelphia bookstore. I turned around, only to find my way blocked by a couple who were examining a book of ghost stories. "You don't believe in that stuff," I asked to break their focus and get past them. But the young man looked at me seriously and said, "I not only believe in it, I work with ghosts!"

A week later, after sunset, four of us were in a car heading towards a road where, according to the other three, the dead Revolutionary Army soldiers of General Washington were pushing up cannons to the hilltop, beyond which lies the Delaware River and its valley: this was the route by which Washington crossed the Delaware and attacked — and defeated — the Hessian mercenaries encamped along the New Jersey side.

My guide and his girlfriend were graduate students in psychology at Temple University. They had invited a medium who had previously made contact with one of the dead soldiers, who identified himself as Robert Tyler. Having gone over the names recorded in the nearby Revolutionary War era cemetery, they found a Robert Taylor and were told that in those days, as it is today, first-generation British immigrants would often pronounce Taylor as Tyler.

We positioned the car at the very bottom of the valley, so that no matter which way we rolled, it would have to be up. I brought along a builder's level and walked both back 50 feet and forward 50 feet to satisfy myself that there was, in fact, an upward incline. It was noticeable to the back, but was minimal forward.

As we waited in the car with the engine off and the gear in neutral, with the windows open, the medium said she felt people approaching. Soon, the car began to move forward and my spine began to tingle with a strange fear. Were we really being pushed along by ghost soldiers?

We didn't go more than ten feet when the young psychologist became quite excited and asked me what I thought of this strange experience. I told him honestly that I was afraid, so he asked the medium to begin speaking with the soldiers. Try as she might, she couldn't get their attention, and in another 25 feet the car halted and the medium said the soldiers had passed us by. My whole body was shaking by now, although the open car window and the cold winter air might have had something to do with it.

I wanted to return in the daylight, to check out the road and its incline, because the three-foot level may not have been accurate on a long road. In any other country, such a place where the car rolls up a hill "by itself" would be called a "magnetic hill." Here, these ghost hunters had a medium's evidence that soldier, dead for 200 years, were at work.

EYE LINE

Ten years later, Dr. Jan Grossman visited me from Philadelphia. I was studying ancient Egypt in Toronto and we had become good friends. He brought his girlfriend and proposed that one evening we perform some mind experiments. I invited a girlfriend and the four of us went through some brain exercises to see if we could raise our awareness to some level of extrasensory perception.

Recently, I had heard the concept that when one concentrates all thoughts and energy through the eyes, there is a "visible" line from his eye to whomever he is looking at. We selected Jan's girlfriend and me to do the experiment of concentration, while Jan and my girlfriend watched from a nearby couch. Jan closed the lights and I looked at the lovely woman not twelve feet before me in the dark. I mentally stirred up all my emotions and imagined this powerful, red beam shining out of my third eye into her heart.

While I may have a good imagination, it was she who achieved results! I began to feel a force pushing at my chest. At first I thought it was cute that this person would be able to manifest enough power of thought or mind to exert a physical force on me, but then the power increased and I was pushed back against the back of my chair! In a moment, no matter how hard I tried to balance myself or resist the force, I knew that I was about to tumble right back, together with my chair, the back of my head most likely to hit the floor first!

"Faith," I called to her, "can you make your gaze gentler?"

She answered very calmly, "No I cannot!"

I was quite struggling by then, and, in desperation, yelled out, "Please look away! Somewhere, anywhere!"

There was an audible crack in the room and Jan yelled out in surprise. He turned on the light and with amazement on his face asked, "What happened?"

My girlfriend crossed her hands over her breasts and hunched down into the sofa, looking up at us suspiciously, but without saying a thing.

"Do you know what you guys just did?" Jan asked, very excited. "This sofa just jumped and hit the wall with the two of us sitting on it!"

My girlfriend nodded in agreement and just looked at us. "It wasn't me," I said. "Faith was just about to push me, chair and all, over to the floor!"

All eyes were on Faith now. She calmly shrugged her shoulders and said, "When Daniel asked me to look away, I looked towards you, Jan, and was going to ask, 'What now?' But I also heard the crack."

We spend hours debating what just happened, and how.

Dr. Grossman and I are still friends, but we never solved this puzzle.

You Never Felt Lonely

Nancy Krieger

I received the following email on March 3, 2010. I hastened to acknowledge receipt of it, and at the same time I expressed my appreciation to Ms. Krieger for having written to me with these four accounts of her family's experiences over the years.

It would seem that perhaps Ms. Krieger and various members of her family, including her skeptical-minded father, are fantasy-prone personalities. Another possibility, that accounts for some of the experiences recorded here, is that members of the family are able to produce poltergeist-like effects (noises, drawers opening and closing, etc.) without knowing they are doing it. There are many such cases on record. A final, way-out-there possibility is that the family has a "familiar" (its own spirit that goes from generation to generation) creating disturbances.

In short, I cannot account for Ms. Krieger's experiences, and I doubt that there is a simple explanation for any or all of them.

Dear Mr. Colombo:

My name is Nancy Krieger and I am a twenty-eight-year-old mother of one. I have lived in the Barrie, Ontario, area my entire life, and after reading a good number of your books, I feel compelled to share some of my stories from over the years. I hope you enjoy them, and if you have any questions regarding any of them, please feel free to email me.

All of the stories I am about to tell have happened to my family over the years. The first of them happened before I was born. The rest are accounts from different so-called haunted houses that I've lived in over my twenty-eight years. Not a single member of my family, not even my father the "skeptic," can say that they haven't had a strange encounter in one of the houses.

SAVING THE BABY

When my mother was an infant in 1958, the entire family was gathered around in the kitchen while my grandmother was cooking dinner. My great grandparents were present at the time also. My mother was on the dining-room table in her baby carrier, when my great grandmother became distraught and began to order my grandmother "Move that baby, now!" After retrieving my mother from the table, an overhead lamp broke for no apparent reason, and the shattered glass landed exactly in the place where my infant mother had been on the table.

THERE'S SOMETHING IN THE ATTIC

In 1987 we moved into a house at 115 Bayfield Street in Barrie, Ontario, that we were renting from my mother's boss. I should mention the house was built sometime in the 1860s.

Including the basement, the house had four storeys, one of which was the attic, but was full size and had two very large bedrooms in it and three crawlspaces for storage. Right after moving in, I began to play in the attic, and instantly began telling my mother of an old man in a gray sweater who played up there with me.

At first my parents passed this off as my imagination, but then one evening a friend, who was staying over at the house, ran out in the middle of the night. When my mother contacted him the next day, he told her he woke in the middle of the night to see an elderly man in a gray sweater yelling in his face, "Get out of my house!"

Shortly after we were settled in, strange noises began to be sounded in the attic, above our bedrooms as we slept. Footsteps, doors closing, coughing, and dragging noises could all be heard throughout the night. My mother was friends with the woman who lived in the house before us, and when she broached the subject, her friend told her that she always felt someone pushing her down the stairs, and that the taps would turn on and off for no reason. No sooner had my mother heard her story than the taps began to turn on full blast in the middle of the night. Not wanting to move out, and with my father a full non-believer, my mother tried to make peace with the spirits by suggesting that they have the attic and that we have the rest of the living space.

After that, all was quiet for a few years, until we began renovations. Shortly thereafter, the noises began again. One evening, when I was a teenager (and sitting in my room avoiding family time, as teens often do), both of my parents were witnesses to a young girl descending the stairs in a flowing white dress. My mother asked where I had gotten the dress from, but as the girl made her way down the stairs, walked past the table my parents were sitting at, and made her way into the basement, it was very apparent that she wasn't me and also wasn't of the living. My mom then promptly looked across the table to my father whose mouth was agape and stated, "Now you can't tell me you didn't see that!"

Footsteps could be heard on our wooden stairs, despite the fact that they were covered in carpet, and often times cold drafts would enter rooms for no reason. We gave up on any renovations, and once we did the disturbances stopped. We learned to live side-by-side with our two ghosts, every now and then taking notice when they would hide something on us or turn a light on or off.

All in all, our ten years in that house were interesting to say the least. You never felt lonely.

On a side note, two weeks after the new tenants had moved in, we received a phone call from them. It was known to us through my mother's boss that the man was turning the attic into an office of sorts, and all I can assume is that our "friends" weren't impressed, because the man asked me very matter of factly, "What is in the attic?"

HAUNTED APARTMENTS

I moved around from place to place between the ages of twenty-one and twenty-six, all within the city of Barrie, however. Many of my apartments were without otherworldly guests, and if I had to admit it, I would say I sort of found it a little bland. One of my apartments, in yet another house that was over a hundred years old, on the other hand, had its fair share of welcome and unwelcome visitors. It was an upper-level apartment, and from the first night my boyfriend at the time and I moved in, strange things began to happen.

The very first morning we woke up in our new place, we found that every door and drawer in the kitchen had been pulled open. We closed them again and went along our way. Two nights later, I woke to go to the washroom and found a young girl standing in front of my front window looking down on the street. Thing is, she was standing in the exact location of my couch, and only the upper half of her body was visible. From then on, whenever I woke in the middle of the night, I forced myself not to look in the direction of the living room, though I could often see her from the corner of my eye.

Five months after we moved in, the people in the downstairs apartment moved out and the landlord had to renovate. So seeing as how it was winter and the place would be empty for a few months, he gave us the key so we could go down and control the heat. One evening, during a particularly bad snowstorm, my boyfriend and I heard the door bang closed downstairs and then footsteps on the hardwood floor. Unsure of whether to call the police or to investigate first, we sat there for a moment and listened. A man's deep voice was heard coughing, and it sounded as though furniture (which there was none of at the time) was being dragged around. My boyfriend armed himself with a baseball bat, as well as the key, and went down to check it out.

When he entered, the entire apartment was empty, and as he exited and walked around the porch, after relocking the door, again the door slammed. This time he bolted around the corner and found nothing but the door that he had just locked. The only set of footsteps in the snow all around the house were his own.

The Visitors

I now live on my own in an older apartment building, with my four-year-old daughter. Though I have never seen anything in the new place, my daughter frequently has conversations with people whom she calls "The Visitors." And I also should mention that once, on a trip to the graveyard to visit my grandfather's grave, when my daughter was about three years old, she struck up conversations there as well.

I didn't tell her what a graveyard was, so as not to startle or upset her. But after laying flowers on the grave, when we were back at the car, my daughter turned and waved and in a very small, innocent voice said, "Goodbye, people."

There have been many more incidents in my life, much like these, but it would take me forever to list them.

All in all these are true accounts and have not been changed in the slightest.

Joanna I Think Her Name Is

Loretta X

My maxim is "do one weird thing a week." The weird thing I did the second-last week of October 2009 was to accept the invitation of Carrie Pierce to address the group that calls itself the Meadowvale Spookies Paranormal Research Team. For the last couple of years, about thirty members of this group have met regularly, usually at the historic site known as The Grange (in Mississauga), which itself is said to be haunted, to discuss ghosts and spirits and how to investigate them. I agreed to speak for an hour or so on the subject of "Ghosts and How to Find Them."

This event took place Saturday afternoon, October 24, 2009, and I had a good time, as did my wife, Ruth, and I hope the other members of MSPRT did too. (Meadowvale is one of the early names of Mississauga, which is part of the Greater Toronto Area.) As I usually do, I invited members of the audience to seek me out and send me their own accounts of paranormal activity for possible use in future books (like this one). A couple of people in the audience were pleased with the invitation and did contact me, including Carrie and, in this instance, Loretta X.

In an email dated October 29, 2009, I heard from Loretta. (That is her real first name; at her request, her last name is given here as X.) Here, somewhat edited for fluency, is her account of being haunted or hazed by a ghost who is named Joanna.

So, in this instance my maxim paid off ... in this instance with Loretta's "spirited" account of Joanna.

Hello John,

Loretta here. I'm the assistant director from the Meadowvale Spookies Paranormal Research Team. It was really nice to meet you and your wife. I hope you had a safe trip home. Here is just one of my stories (experiences) that I told you I would send you. Hope you could use it. Here is my story:

This is a true story about a young girl named Loretta, that's me. And a female spirit. I moved into a house with my parents when I was a teenager in Brampton, Ontario. It all started with a photo on the wall of my niece and nephew. It was crooked when I came downstairs. So I fixed it. And went on with my day.

A few days went by and again the same photo of my niece and nephew was crooked. I fixed it again. Then almost every day after that the same photo of my niece and nephew was crooked the same way, every day. I called to my mother and said, "Do you or dad keep moving this photo of the kids?"

She said no and then said, "Why would you ask me that?"

I said, "It's been crooked every time I came downstairs in the morning, and look at all the other photos on the wall. They are all straight!"

"Oh, don't worry about it, Loretta," my mother said. "You're going to be late for school."

One night I went to bed late. I got in to my bed and turned off the light, got all comfy and warm. Then I heard someone say my name. I sat up and looked around … no one was there! Maybe I'm hearing things, I said to myself, so I went to sleep.

A few days later I got into bed again, and this time something touched my leg! It was rubbing the lower part of my leg! I shook my leg and thought, "What was that?" I had no answer and went to sleep.

About this time I started to have nightmares of nuclear war and the aftermath, with zombies walking around trying to get me. The next night a zombie came into my room, sat on my bed, and touched my leg again. "Am I going crazy?" I asked myself. So you would hear things during the day, like someone going up or down the stairs, cupboards opening and closing, doors too. There is someone talking, but I can't quite hear them.

Then one night I got out of bed to use the bathroom. Got to the bathroom, looked into my parents' room, and saw a blacker-than-black shadow person. It was looking at my parents and about to touch one of them. Then it slowly turned its head and looked at me!

It had white glowing eyes like flashlights, but without the beam coming from the lights. It stood up and I ran into the bathroom as fast as I could, flicked the light on, and stood there waiting for it to come and get me. Nothing happened and I fell asleep in the washroom.

Two nights went by and it was time for bed again. I turned off the light, closed and opened my eyes a few times, and there it was standing in my doorway, as tall as the doorway, as black as night, with those white glowing eyes. "Shit!" I said, and pulled the blankets over my head, reached for the lamp on the bedside table, and turned it on. I stayed under there for what seemed to be an eternity. Then I fell asleep.

The next day I sat my mother down and asked her what had happened in the house. "What are you talking about, Loretta?" she said.

So I told her about all of what was happening to me. First she tried to tell me it was my father checking on me. "Mom," I said, "Dad is not 6–7 feet tall and he doesn't have white glowing eyes! Now, what happened?"

She started to tell me that when she first came upon the property, she knew something had happened there too. Someone was killed in the house, she told me.

"Who?" I said.

She went upstairs and came down with a piece of newspaper. It said a young woman was killed by her husband. She was stabbed 14 or 27 times, or something like that. But they had two small children, a boy and a girl, the same age as my niece and nephew in the photo on the wall! The man went to jail. The kids went to live with a brother of the killer.

Talking with the people who lived next door, I asked them why they were moving, just having a baby and all. They told us that they see her (Joanna, I think her name is) in our back yard and the wife can't handle it. You know, having the baby and all. "Oh, I see," we said.

So then I just got used to her. Joanna would move things in front of me. I would see her night or day. One time I saw her as an all-white figure. I could see her face, dress, and even the holes in her body from the knife. She sat in my room every night until I fell asleep.

Then, one day, I went to a party at a friend's place. I meet a man who told me he has to talk to me about the ghost in my house. He told me how to help her. So I did what he told me to do.

I never saw her. Now, in my life, I can see, talk to, hear, feel, smell, etc., them. And, yes, more things have happened.

Thank you for taking the time to read my true-life story. I am well seasoned in the realm of metaphysics and "ghost hunting." I am interested and dedicated to this line of work! Through investigations, research, experiments, and studies, I will find my truth to the mysteries of the paranormal world.

Ghost Story of Dr. Lionel Macklin

Eric Macklin

I owe the title is this section to Eric Macklin (Ret.), who divides his time between Toronto and Barrie, Ontario. (What Mr. Macklin is retired from, I do not know.) This email Macklin sent me on July 13, 2009. It is written with considerable wit, and the word "ingenious" is the one to use, to describe its various arguments about the psychology of perception. Anyway, here is what Mr. Macklin (Ret.) wrote.

I am currently working my way through one of your books, *The Midnight Hour*. Been a great believer of ghost stories and ran into a few myself ... quite educational to say the least ... most don't want to be disturbed and quietly go about their business ... some actually acknowledge your presence ... their option of course ... thought I'd send one of my along ... hope you enjoy it....

Ghost Story of Dr. Lionel Macklin
York Apartments Revisited — Again

Prelude

Ghost stories, as we all know, have been around in varying degrees and disguises for well over three thousand years. Some ghosts and their "stories" of course are better known than others. Phrases like "figments of their / our imaginings," ghost stories of ghosts returning in various forms for various and sundry reasons, known only unto themselves, to their favourite "haunts," which take the shape in a thousand and one forms and places down through history and into modern times. Ghosts, as it would seem, dwell amongst us in various plantasmic / extoplasmic / protoplasmic / electronically detectable shapes, some more-or-less, well-or-better defined in appearance if that be the case, or of simple presences depending on the wants and needs and desires of both the ghostee and the hostee. And of course some stories, recalling of these interactions, whether visual, sensual in its many versions, and of course in more modern times, as detected by all sorts of electrical devices.

The next question that we must deal with, and this is of course for both the believer and non-believer to deal with, and that is, do ghosts in their many forms, do they really exist? Absolutely and without a doubt. And furthermore, I can prove it to you right now, and furthermore do it personally. And I can prove it from your own personal experiences with your very own ghost.

Let me first of all preference my proof with this thought derived from the foregoing paragraph. Ghosts, for the most part, are derived from their "presences" in time and space. That is they, in order to be ghosts, must have existed, if only for a short time. They lived, they breathed, they walked around, they did stuff just like you and me. And we all know that the body we live in today is run on 80% water and a host of other minerals and sugars that create an electrolyte similar in many ways to a battery of sorts. We all had fun by over-charging our little electrolyte battery by wearing slippers of various sorts and scuffing them across the rug, especially on a dry day and discharging the "charge" by placing our mischievous finger on our kid sister or brother to watch them yelp on the receiving end.

So then, having proven that we have electrolytes and that we have an electro-charged body, we move on to the next step in our little experiment. Our very own ghost. Have you ever seen, on TV or YouTube, time-lapse photography? Of course you have. So here we go, as your body moves through time and space within your surroundings, your body will leave little time-lapse photography impressions on its environment, much like the "flicks" of olde movies. The smoother the movie, the faster the "flickering." In the old days, we watched TV which was nothing more than an oscilloscope and we watched it in black and white. Hence, ghosts for the older generation are in some form of black and white. As we moved into the age of colour, our recalled experiences tended to move into the realm of colour as well, which by necessity included our dreams. This will also include our experiences with ghosts.

Ah yes. I did mention your very own ghost. Let me not prolong the suspense. Keep in mind the previous paragraph and the ultra-low technology of the "flicker / flicka" footprint that we are constantly leaving in our lives. Have you ever (we all have) experienced the times when you think of doing something one moment and then, with life's little interruptions, completely forget what it was you were about to do? We all have. Have you ever spent a few minutes, even, on occasion, a few more minutes of trying to figure out just what is was you were about to do? Something really important, but "it just slipped your mind." So there you are reading this, and I am leaning over in my armchair and looking you, the reader, straight in the eye (the mind's eye of course) and saying, "Go ahead, admit it, hundreds of times … right?" Sure you have. So then, what have you done to shorten the time to figure out what your poor brain came up with for you to do and taken so intermediately long to figure out. Feeling a little less intuitive are we. What's that old / new phrase … "Bin der, dun dat."

Okay, my friend, enter the "flicker / flicka" technology driven by your very own body's electrolytes. The thought about doing something came to you in a previous time-space-moment, a few steps back-space in your life as you walked from one locale or one room to another locale or room, or even in your car / bike / moped further down the road. You have moved on, as they say. And you have "forgotten" what the hell it was that was so damn important just a few seconds / moments ago that you just had to do. The will all the forgoing, here's the secret:

1. The first step is to stop where you are and ask yourself what it was that you wanted to do. That much we have all done and for the most part to no avail. Nothing happens. Zip, Nada, nothing, complete blank.

2. The second step, ready for this are we, as you my friend are about to meet and very near and dear, very close personal friend of yours, none other than YOU. Yep, YOU. To be totally honest here, one of the many "flicka-YOUs."

3. Step back, peddle back, ride back to where your body's electrolytes first lit the magic bulb of inspiration and thought of that more-or-less great idea that set you in motion to go do that important-enough-something that moved your feet in the direction of whatever the hell it was to do. If it was in the other room, then go back and stand in the same place, or as close as possible to where it was when the "idea" arrived. Then, before you even try to ask yourself just what exactly was it that you wanted to do, it pops back into your mind ... and off you go to do it again.

Those of you who are intuitive enough (in tune with things around you) already know the answer as to where the idea was "sent again" (your tele-receptors were turned on and working) to the mind's eye and picked out of the air, this time *air* is spelt "aire," that magical ether of "time and space." You my friend have just met your very own ghost. One of thousands of "ectoplasmic imprints or footprints" left behind to be found by either yourself or others at a later date. Some of course more memorable than others.

What others are left to see are of course the more memorable "footprints" that your protoplasm has left behind as an "ectoplasm signature," due to either emotions, fear, happiness, the whole panache of emotions that we experience through our electrolytes and leave behind. Note the combination of the two words "ectoplasm" and "signature" — together they are your very own "ghostly figure," which you have just been introduced to in this prelude to the story of the ghost of Dr. Lionel Macklin and the York Apartments. It does, and more importantly, still exists.

GHOST STORY OF DR. LIONEL MACKLIN
(A CASE STUDY)

Our story begins, or shall I say our retelling of an occurrence on a "continuing basis" of course, as there are many here, in this fashion. Ghosts, like so many ghosts, are just like us, but are now mere shadows of their former self, of course, to rephrase an old idiom, and are out there, in they're simply doing what they've always done, just puttering around. But, and there are always a few of those, some ghosts have left a more lasting impression of ectoplasmic than others, for one reason or another.

The other "aspect" of the "ghostee and hostee" interface / interplay / interaction is that we must have our antennae up, or be receptive or intuitive, whatever it is that is required to be cognitive of their presence(s). There are lots of times and places where we as "ghostee and hostee" simply pass each other without any intuitive knowledge of each other's presence. That doesn't mean in any way that they don't exist. One of the parties is just too busy doing something else.

In terms of the *raison d'être* of this piece about the ghost of one Dr. Lionel Macklin, storied physician of the small southern Ontario town of Stratford and environs, is the occasional occurrence of the presence of the good doctor and pediatrician in and around his medical office, situated on the lower floor at the north end of the olde York Apartments across from the olde bandshell and park by the Avon River.

The building today is much as it was in the 1930s to the 1950s when Dr. Macklin ran his practice there, with his well-known, lit shingle hanging off the corner of the building as he worked on occasion late into the night. Today, the north entrance is now bricked up and the concrete steps removed, much to the dismay of the ghost I am sure, with a new entrance to the office, now a little apartment, from the inside just to the left of the main entrance, with "103" affixed to the door. The elevator is still the same period piece as it was during the 1930s, with the sliding door and spring-loaded brass gate, much like the childproof gates of old and today.

As it just so happened, I was down visiting my brothers in Stratford on May 29th, 2002, to celebrate my father's birthday. He would have been celebrating his 100th birthday. As part of the nostalgia of the day I decided to visit the site of my father's olde office and have a walk through the olde York Apartment block to reacquaint myself, as it were, with old times and memories of my father and the things we did as kids. Leaving home, visiting Dad with a friend, off to the Vogue Theater for a show, then after across the street to the Jumbo Ice Cream Store for a "box" of ice cream (not the cone). From here we would visit Dad again and then go next door to buy a pop from the Kist Canada Company and watch the bottling process as they made our pop and we took a couple off the assembly line.

Visiting Dad of course always meant picking up a quarter for whatever was in our agenda for the next little while. From there we would visit his mother, my grandmother, for milk and cookies, and then head home for supper. As you can tell on those Saturday routines, we were not generally hungry and Dad covered for us, as was his want. The only variance here was that on occasion we would go to the Avon Theater and fill up on peanuts from the Nut Club across the street during the intermissions. At show's end, we would head home and play cowboys and Indians all the way home and across the "flats." Either way we still weren't hungry for supper. And dad covered for us yet again. We were *simpatico*, one would say. We were "in tune."

So there I was that fateful day in 2002, at the front door of the York Apartments, and having made sure that I had parked my car pointed at the olde entrance, again just like the old days. I was, sort of knowingly, lining myself up for the "reunion," and what a reunion it was. At last "ghostee" and "hostee" were in sync or were *simpatico*, a sort of Vulcan mind-meld as it were; we were face to face, and the beauty of it all was that we acknowledged each other. A pivotal moment to be sure. Dad was wearing his suit, and in his lapel was a small white rose reminiscent of all the rose shows he won around Perth County. Just inside, to the left of the entrance of the building, was a small table by the little window, also with white roses and a small chair to the left of that again, just outside the new door to Apartment 103.

You can't talk to ghosts, but you can see them, and in watching them carefully you can detect other means of simple communication such as gestures and body language. And no, we can't use Braille. What I noticed first of all, after our recognition moment, was that he seemed to be aware of "his" new entrance to his office as being through that new door. He asked via gestures that I should sit in the little chair, and through my mind's eye we visited his office, just as it had been years ago. His desk, his chair, the filing cabinet, the cigarette smoke rising from the heavy green glass ashtray, all in front of me, and the green tiled fireplace just behind me all aglow. Funny I don't ever remember it working. But there it was.

Another thing that caught my eye was the fact that even ghost doctors have their patients. In his case they were small kids. Ah yes, Dad ("Bud") was a pediatrician. How they got there is and was not my concern, but they were local kids who had for one reason or another slipped over to the other side. All I can say is that they are well looked after. The office equipment was much as it has always been, the old mercury sun-lamp, the electric scalpels, the scopes, the oscilloscope, which was fairly new, and the neat old centrifuge that I used to play with when I was there. What still hung from my Dad's belt was his personal black scalpel pack. The interface, I am sure, lasted only a few minutes, including a run up to the fourth floor in the olde elevator for one reason or another to Apartment 403. Why he went up there, I have no idea, maybe another year another visit. As it turns out, in 2006, an old friend of his was sick.

A few minutes later, it was, as it always is, with slight variations, it all ended and I awoke in that chair. All was well with the world, I felt a little more at peace. The next few moments were truly enlightening and reconfirming in so many gentle ways. As I returned to my locked car, I opened the door, and there, resting ever so gently on the driver's seat, was a single white petal from a white rose bush. In the years that followed since then, another petal would appear from a white rose bush or a white peace rose bush.

EPILOGUE

There are numerous variations since then, but one really intrigued me, and that was that the new home we now have up here in Barrie since 2007 came with a white rose bush that was not doing that well. The following year, in 2008, and after my annual visit to York apartments and Dad, the rose seemed to thrive. To add to that was the fact that, unprompted, my eldest son, who now lives in Newmarket, planted a single white rose bush in his front garden, which is also thriving. Odd? ... maybe, we'll soon see. Maybe ghosts travel as well; I'll have to check that out with Dad the next time I "see" him.

I corresponded further with Mr. Macklin, of course, and in the process I learned two facts. The first is that the correspondent uses "Ret." in parentheses to refer to his status as "retired" from one line of work or another, "but not dead" — retired from life. The second of these facts is that the correspondent had another story at hand, one told in his inimitable style, which I read with avid interest. As I have his permission to use this story, as well as the earlier one, here goes....

Good evening John:

This is a true story. My wife's uncle's name has been altered for various reasons. She asked me to write this one down as it really disturbed her. I was joking about Rob but she wasn't the least bit amused. Some people are more "in tune" than others. And it was a tad humorous as well, but not to her. Most of my family was dead when I was young, so she thinks I am wired for this "connection." Nothing like Jennifer Love-Hewitt's character though.

BARRIE
GHOST STORY OF ROBERT FINDLAY
LAKE OF BAYS COTTAGE REVISITED — AGAIN

PRELUDE

Ghost stories, like many stories, come in all manner of shapes and sizes, and some are more detailed than others. While they can be humorous to some, they can be truly terrifying to others, or at the very least certainly unsettling, as they say. The story I am about to relay to you, the reader, requires a little background in order to provide the *raison d'être* as to why the ghost appears, or more properly in this instance, the spirit of one dearly departed individual. In this "instance," the individual ghost's name was Robert Findlay (name changed just a tad to protect the innocent).

Robert or "Rob," as he was known for the better part of his 90+ years wondering amongst us, was born in east side Toronto, grew up there, and was fighter pilot *extraordinaire* during the war, flying Corsairs. Out of all of this came a young man who was meticulous in every detail, neat as a pin goes the iconic phrase, and if you ever needed any help, just ask. That was the operative verb that ruled his life, and God help those who crossed his path and didn't "fly" by his rules. Hence our story, as I failed to do so even after his untimely death (aren't they all) two years ago at the age of 90, in a spring canoeing accident up at the lake. He was an accomplished canoer, like myself. The incident I am about to describe occurred two years later. We should have known better.

When we first started to go up to our cottage each year, we all, as I am sure there are others with a similar experience all over cottage country, had to turn on the electricity and ultimately hook up the water supply. After all, this is why they call it "cottage country," septic tank systems and all. So there I was, the rookie starting to "hook up the cottage," following some rather dubious instructions from the previous family owner. Open the valve, pour in some water, let it gurgle, and then plug in the water pump. Sounds familiar, sure enough. And Rob Findlay was there to supervise, as his cottage was next door. Five times we did this and nothing was happening, then Rob stepped outside, as the effort was inside of course, and heard the water we were pouring all this time down the pipe, trickling down the pipe and out the other end and leaking back into the well, just outside where we couldn't hear it.

Laughter ensued and two more beers. "Ah yes," he said. "I just remembered that you, the lucky new cottage owner of a 50+ year-old cottage, forgot to hook up the two pipe ends in the well. One to the cottage and one to the lake."

"Sure, why not indeed," I said.

Thank God I asked for Rob's help, hell I probably would have spent the whole day pouring water down the drain, literally, till I had it figured out … maybe. So, each spring, as I hooked the water system up, getting faster and better each year, Rob would come by and reminisce about that spring in 1999 when I made my first try. And a few more beers.

Part One

Our story begins like all stories (gotta start somewhere) for Robert (Rob) Findlay in the late spring of 2009, and the cottage had already been opened up. No problems there. I was putting the dock in, which comes in two pieces, the dock itself and the walk out, a fairly ubiquitous set up for Muskoka cottagers. A couple of the concrete blocks had broken due largely to ice and simple wear and tear. As a result, I bought a couple of new 10-inch blocks from our local supplier and carefully placed them in the water to support the dock. But then I needed "just one more 6 inch block," and what was to become, like in any story, the "causative incident." I knew that just next door, Uncle Rob, through my wife's family, had a couple. Soooo, I wandered over like a good neighbour to Uncle Rob's cottage and "took" one. Huge mistake. Yep, didn't deem to ask the dearly departed if I could "borrow" one. The new concrete block safely in place, I returned to the cottage for lunch.

Part Two

Okay, can you feel it coming? Rob, the most excellent squadron wingman and gunner had me, his long time paddling buddy, in his sights. I had no sooner stepped into the cottage, when my lovely wife mentioned that there was something amiss with the water pump, as it was surging, which meant that the two water pipe ends in the well head had come apart. Now wasn't that odd, and at just that precise moment. The water system had "malfunctioned." Just like that. I looked at my wife, she looked at me, and ... all I could think of was Uncle Rob. I had forgot the operative verb and threw in a few borrowed from fellow Irishman. Obviously, a big mistake. I joked about it to my Scottish wife and she turned as white as a ... you guessed it.

So, back to the dock, I removed the offending piece of concrete and took it back to the exact place I had borrowed it from and returned to the cottage and dutifully reconnected the water pipes. Ah yes, Rob was Irish, and of course it didn't end there, not by a long shot. With the water lines fixed, I came up to the kitchen and said the coast was clear; we were cool with Rob. Not quite. The circuit in the kitchen flickered and went "dead." Two new outlets later and a new junction box, I had it fixed two hours later. But I had a hunch Rob wasn't quite through with me yet, and I clearly had him in my mind; and on it went.

It started to rain, and it came right though the roof into the kitchen. That day an old branch had hit the roof, just after the concrete block incident. So, after the rain stopped, and buckets were cleared away, and a trip to Home Depot, I went up on the roof and fixed the shingle and the small split in the "gutter." No problem, my brother just happened to come by and lend me hand. He went home, and thanked me for my call. I looked at my wife, and she looked at me, and we told him we knew nothing of any phone call. We thought it was odd, as he left, then it hit us, Uncle Rob was getting his pound of flesh for not asking for that piece of concrete.

And Rob was still not finished. Suddenly, the hot water heater was giving us the "cold treatment," so I replaced the fuses and plugged the unit back into the fuse box, at which point the whole cottage "went dead." I got that distinct feeling from Uncle Rob that he was screwing with me still, saying, "Can you hear me now?" as I replied, "Oh yah." We called the electrician in and he said that the power was out in the area, and then we all sat back and laughed.

Later, after diner, I looked up into the sky and asked Uncle Rob if I could have that piece of concrete, and for some strange reason I could see and hear him say, "Why sure, now that you asked."

The cottage has been fine ever since. Uncle Rob may never have appeared as a "ghost," but he was there nonetheless. I can hear him laughing still. If you don't believe me, just "ask" him.

Now if I could just find his lost canoe, he'd be really happy.

THE HAUNTING OF TABER HILL PARK

Jacqui Medeiros

I have never seen a ghost or a spirit, but I have often felt that places are "haunted" or are somehow "special."

The first time I set eyes on Taber Hill Park, which is a municipal park in the middle of Scarborough, a residential area in the east end of Toronto, I felt it to be "special" in that sense. The park is essentially a mound that rises 174 metres above Lake Ontario and 14 metres above the street level. Residential streets in the vicinity bear such Native-influenced names as Indian Mound Crescent, Longhouse Place, and Rochman Boulevard.

The mound itself is a natural formation, covered with grass and crowned with a grey granite boulder with a bronze plaque. The plaque explains that the site is an ancient ossuary of the Iroquois nation. Burials were made here in about 1250 A.D. The ossuary was first uncovered when farmlands were developed into residential properties in 1956, and the park was dedicated as an historical site on October 21, 1961.

I featured the site in words and photographs in my book *Haunted Toronto*, which was published in 1996. Up to that time, nobody had ever regarded it as more than an ossuary. I felt it to be a "vision site" that was used by Iroquois braves for their initiation into the warrior clan. (I feel the same way about two other historic sites: Peterborough Petroglyphs and Serpent Mounds, north and south of the city of Peterborough, Ontario.)

Tabor Hill Park has an odd feel to it, and over the years I have taken visitors to the site, and they too have found that it seems "strange." When I climb the mound, what comes to my mind is Frank Lloyd Wright's architectural principle "compression leading to expansion." There is not much on ground level except road traffic. The climb is a lonely one. At the summit of the mound, one's consciousness or at least awareness of the atmosphere and the environment expands, and the climber may survey much of Scarborough, including churches, schools, hospitals, health-care facilities, and high-tension power-lines. It is a place of healing and of power.

The park's name recalls the biblical Mount Tabor, where the newly risen Christ appeared to his disciples as a figure "transfigured." The city employee who named the park in the 1950s probably had this passage from the New Testament in mind. Indeed, the skyline of Taber Hill in Scarborough amazingly recalls the silhouette of Mount Tabor, near the Sea of Galilee in Israel.

In a public talk on ghosts and spirits of Toronto at the Canadian National Exhibition on August 17, 2009, I devoted a few sentences to a description of the park, stressing that there is no tradition of the locale being haunted by a ghost, but that the site does convey the sense of being the habitat of a spirit — a ghost being the personality of a deceased person, a spirit being the embodiment of some force or power. I went on to discuss some of the city's haunted houses, including Old Fort York, Mackenzie House, and Courtroom 33 of the Old Toronto City Hall.

After the talk, about half a dozen members of the audience approached me to share with me their own experiences with haunted sites in the city. Among the sharers was Jacqui Medeiros, who immediately caught my attention when she said she lives on Painted Post Drive in the vicinity of "Indian Mound," the popular designation of Taber Hill, which is indeed circled by Indian Mound Crescent. She told me she believes the place to be haunted. When I expressed considerable interest, she offered to send me an account of her experiences. I urged her to do so through my website; I promised to send her one of my books in exchange.

Returning home from the CNE, I realized I should have asked Ms. Medeiros for her email address! So, all I could do was cross my fingers and hope that she would remember her promise. Happily she did! Her account, reproduced here as she wrote it and as I received it on September 5, 2009, makes for exciting reading. I replied by email, thanking her ... and assuring her that one of my recent "ghost books" would shortly be winging its way to her as soon as she sent me her mailing address!

Good evening,

My name is Jacqui Medeiros, and I met you last week at the CNE after your Thursday discussion on Toronto hauntings. I introduced myself to you after your speech and told you I lived on Painted Post near Indian Mound (I think you called it Taber Park?) that you had mentioned in your talk.

We have had at least 10 actual sightings of native people, always men, in our basement. They have been seen by myself, my daughter (who is now 13), and a glimpse once by my son (now 12). Sometimes they are accompanied by a musty smell. Always, they set off my dog since we got him 5 years ago.

Our dog, Panda, is a 5-year-old Shih Tzu who spends most of his time in the basement, where his bed is, his food, etc. He is a pretty calm dog and only gets excited if he hears someone at our door, outside our house, etc. He's not a yappy kind of dog. However, when one of our "visitors," as we call them, decides to pop in, he gets very agitated. He stares at the place that my daughter or I can see the apparition and growls or barks in anger. This is very unusual behaviour unless there is a stranger (i.e., the water-metre reader) coming into the house. Even when we can't see anything, he will sometimes growl in that general area of our basement (at the foot of the stairs) for no apparent reason.

One day while walking Panda, the children and I decided to go to Indian Mound for a different route. Panda would not even go to the base of it. I was tugging on his leash and he started barking at the mound like crazy. I was curious so I picked him up (he's only about 15 pounds) and took him up the hill.

At the top of the hill, my daughter started feeling uneasy. She is what I call a "sensitive." She feels, sees, and hears things that most people don't. Anyway, she said she had to get off of this hill, that there was something here she wasn't happy about, and it was making her sick. She left the mound and crossed the street.

Panda knew he did not have the freedom to just get off the hill himself, so he just sat down, unhappily, and pouted until I took him down. Then once on the sidewalk across the street, he turned to face the hill, barked furiously for about 30 seconds, then turned tail and pulled on the leash as hard as he could to get out of there.

We've never returned to Indian Mound since that day, although we've had a few "visitors" since then in our basement. I'm personally convinced it is related.

I Started to Have Strange Experiences

Jennifer Meloche

I received the following letter, which was very carefully printed on lined paper by post on June 10, 2009. The letter itself is dated March 16, 2009. The correspondent, Jennifer Meloche, is unknown to me, but she is the kind of person I would like to meet, for she writes with clarity and she takes pains to distinguish between what she has experienced and what her readers will think about her and her impressions when they read about these three experiences.

As a matter of course, I wrote to Ms. Meloche, who does not use email, and asked her to check over the printout of this account. I also asked her for some biographical information. Here is her reply.

As far as biographical information, I have never done that before, so here is what I have and if it is too long or needs changing, by all means go for it!

My name is Jennifer Meloche. I am a homemaker, who was born in the winter of 1974. I live in Leamington, Ontario, Canada, with my husband of 8 years, Randy Meloche, and our 3 young sons.

When I am not chasing the boys, I enjoy writing, reading, gardening, and the outdoors, whether it's camping, hiking, or just enjoying the peace and serenity of my favourite yearly vacation spot on Pelee Island.

Because of my experiences, I have always been quite interested in the supernatural + spirit world and am always looking for other great stories with those similar experiences.

I thank you so much for this opportunity and look forward to hearing from you in the future.

I have no explanations for any of these eerie occurrences because I do not feel that events and experiences like these may be readily explained. The third account that is recorded here is particularly interesting for the reason that there does seem to be a reason why the effects occurred, assuming that violent acts in the past are somehow remembered or even re-enacted in the present and presumably in the future as well.

I am a true believer in life after death and I am glad to know that there are others out there who have had experiences, just as I have. While my stories are not of any famous buildings or houses, they did really happen and I am glad to share them with someone who won't judge me on how crazy I may sound.

Growing up I lived in an old red brick "farm" house about a quarter mile outside town limits. While I can't quite remember the exact age when I started to have strange experiences, I'll guess that I was pre-teen to teen years.

My first experience happened one evening in my bedroom. I'll describe to you that my bed sat against the wall opposite my closet, and that I never left my closet door open. However, on this particular night, I forgot to close it. Now to the story. I was in bed reading and started to grow tired, so I set my book down, rolled over and turned out my light. Shortly after that, I rolled back and opened my eyes, only to see an older woman in a lacy white, floor-length gown with a veil staring back at me, from the closet. She was as clear as day, only I could see the wall through her. I was so frightened that I flipped the light on, and she was gone. Once I regained motor skills, I got out of bed and closed the door. Needless to say, I never forgot to close it again.

My second experience happened upstairs as well. I was downstairs in the kitchen getting ready to go outside, when I realized I forgot to get my sweater. So, up the twelve steps I went to the top and stopped dead in my tracks. There, about ten steps away from me, with arms folded across his chest, standing in front of my bedroom door, was what I describe as an Indian warrior. Unlike the first spirit, for some reason I was not afraid of this one, maybe a little startled though.

He was the most amazing sight. His hair, black as a raven, flowed down his back. His headdress was made of feathers and a stripe of hide that went over his forehead. On his face, he had some kind of ceremonial paint. His pants looked to be made of some kind of brown hide with fringes and beading going down the outside of the pant legs. He wore no shoes and had a long wooden pole which rested in the folds of his arms. As I took it all in, he then turned and disappeared. At that point, I took off running down the stairs, forgetting about my sweater.

My third experience. I was not alone and no spirit was seen, but we sure had a "creepy" experience. I will start this one by saying that our kitchen ceiling is higher than the archway of the door which leads to the hallway. Once in the hall, you go right and up six steps, then a little turn right again and up six more steps to the top. There are four bedrooms, and mine was the second door on the left. My neighbour and good friend was over.

My brother had received a helium balloon from an event he had been to, and we were messing around with it in the kitchen. At one point, the balloon, which was at the ceiling, lowered and went through the archway, into the hall, then proceeded to float up the stairs through the hall and fell to the floor in front of my bedroom door. My girlfriend and I started laughing and figuring the air was just running low. We thought, let's try again and see what happens. So, back in the kitchen to see what would happen. Sure enough, but to our surprise, we followed the balloon on the same path it had taken minutes before. Only difference this time, we left the balloon where it was and ran down the stairs and out of the house. I guess the first time was fine but the second was definitely not a coincidence.

As if this letter isn't long enough, I hope you don't mind hearing another one. I promise it's not as long. My sister lives in Stratford, Ontario, Canada, and I was down there for a visit in March of 2005 or 2006. Her boyfriend at the time was renting a very old farm house on Embro Road. They wanted me to check out the renovations he had done. So one evening we headed there.

I Started to Have Strange Experiences

The old house is set back in from the road. We stepped inside and I got a tour of the main floor and the basement. From there we went up a set of stairs. Upstairs there are three bedrooms and a half-bathroom. Once at the top of the stairs, you turn right a bit and walk down a hall. At the end of the hall is the bath. Before that, there are two bedrooms on the left. We looked inside the first room and then as we proceeded (my sister in front of me) to the second room, I was overcome with a strong emotion of sadness. I almost went to the floor and I was literally in tears. My sister turned to see what was wrong and truthfully couldn't tell her. I had no idea what was happening to me. She proceeded into the third bedroom where her boyfriend was and let him in on what was happening to me.

Once I gained my composure and went to where they were, they began to tell me that long, long ago a child or children died or were killed in the first bedroom, and that a woman hanged herself or was hanged in the second bedroom. I guess if you are outside and look up at the window you can see the woman standing there, looking out.

To this day I still don't know what happened to me that night, and nothing like that has happened since. But the one thing you can count on is I'll never forget the night I was brought to tears for no reason at all.

Now I Know I'm Not Crazy

Rosa Monti

I received the following email on November 19, 2010, from a woman who has identified herself as Rosa Monti. I am tempted to state that Mrs. Monti's account speaks for itself. At the same time, a few comments are in order.

As this account shows, in the incident recorded, the writer was plainly upset, as was one of her daughters, so the scene is charged with high emotion. Do emotions let loose supernatural powers? Are we especially accessible to the energies of ghosts and the powers of spirits when emotions run high? This account would suggest that this explanation is so.

Curious about the "ghost whisperer," I emailed Mrs. Monti to request more details. Her reply has been worked into the present account. "I think it is important for us to share our experiences with the other side. I was a doubting Thomas, but now I have no choice ... I have to believe the unbelievable. When I think back to all that has happened in my life, and my brushing them away with false LOGIC, I feel sorry for the entities who were trying to break through. I now welcome them with an open heart."

Hello, Mr. Colombo, I'm not regularly visited by unknown beings, but I only started to believe that they exist a few years ago. I'm somewhat over 50 years old, a professional (science and math being my background), so I've always tried to explain past "events" with LOGIC.

It's been about 3 years since my last episode. It started in January–February of 2008. My eldest daughter was experiencing severe anxiety and panic attacks when faced with university and its implications. She had gone from an honour role to "impossible to attend" school. The day she received her first year's university honour-role award, she decided to quit school altogether.

We consulted with social services, doctors, and psychologists. Every one of them found nothing wrong. "Just snap out of it," they said.

Needless to say, she received my husband's and my unconditional support throughout. It was at the time that we had exasperated all medical opinions that the footsteps began.

We live on a multi-level home. I sleep separately from my hubby (I snore), on the lower level from everyone else. Just above my bedroom is where my troubled daughter's bedroom sits.

It had been a long while since I would awake at 3:00 a.m., every morning, like clockwork. There was a clip, clip, clip.... It woke me every night. I didn't think much about it at first. The first time I noticed a "strangeness" was in January–February, just before my daughter's full-blown panic set in. The clips became footsteps starting in my youngest daughter's bedroom, and then the passageway, between the two girls' room, and then my husband's, and finally in my eldest daughter's.

From then on, they only happened in my oldest daughter's room. The three footsteps above my head become increasingly stronger ... always 3 steps from the doorway towards where her bed lies. Days turned into weeks, and weeks turned to months. Every night those footsteps would creep towards her bed.

During that time, my daughter stopped attending school, couldn't work, and usually spent her days on my lap asking me if she was going mad. At night I'd find her curled up at the foot of my bed crying for help. I was at my wit's end and prayed for guidance, and started to believe that there was some sort of evil entity in my home. Boy, did I pray! That's the last thing I could ever have imagined myself doing.

I finally decided to stay awake one night and find out if the steps I heard were true or were a dream occurrence. True to form, there they were: 3:30 a.m. I cursed at them and told them to get the hell out of my house.

Within seconds I could feel something grab my throat. I sat on my bed thinking that this would be the end of me. I couldn't cry for help or anything. I just remember thinking and screaming (mentally) that they had better get the hell out of my home, that they didn't scare me, and then I started to pray to God for help.

The choking stopped. The footsteps were back upstairs, 3 steps from my eldest daughter's doorway, making their way to her bed. Soon after, they were in my youngest daughter's room. They crept from her doorway to her bed, then out the door and towards my husband's room. Just before his doorway, I heard a loud thump; no, it was thunder. It vibrated and shook the house.

For days I couldn't function and even cancelled most of my appointments. I've been practising for over 20 years and have never missed an appointment or disappointed my customers. But I couldn't function rationally anymore.

Two days later, I was lead to the truth. I had heard of a ghost whisperer who had helped an acquaintance, and asked for help. Without giving him any details, he entered my home and went through each room, not sensing anything concrete. That's until he got to my husband's doorway. He said he felt something, but he wasn't sure what it was. We sat downstairs a while, but he kept getting up and going to the spot where I heard the bang. He did this quite a few times, but couldn't understand the sensation and assumed whatever it was now gone or chased out by someone or something else. Since the positive entity was an elderly woman, the only explanation we came up with was that my maternal grandmother was protecting us. During troubled times I felt her. This time she just came on a little bit stronger, I guess. Maybe she got rid of the negative entity.

To give you a little background on the house: We purchased an older home in the late 1980s and tore it down. During the meetings and transaction with the old owners, they always spoke of their two children, a boy and a girl, and how wonderful and happy a time they had had in the home. It was a great neighbourhood and they were sure we would enjoy bringing up our own children here. The girls were aged one and two when we moved in.

During the first few years in our new home, I'd do the laundry and hang the clothes in our unfinished basement. The crying started almost immediately. Without fail, every time I would go downstairs to hang the clothes, I'd hear a child cry and sobbing. I'd rush up 4 flights of stairs only to find the girls sleeping peacefully. The crying stopped after we finished the basement. It wasn't until my daughter's episodes that I remembered the child's cries and every time I thought of the old owners and their children, I always thought "three" and never the "two" they claimed to have raised in the house. I couldn't explain why I always thought "three," never "two."

My neighbour has been living next door for the last 60 years, and when I asked her about the previous owners and their children, she said, "Yes, they had two living children, as the oldest daughter committed suicide when she was 18." That sent shivers up and down my spine, as my daughter's panic and anxiety had started when she was 18. It's also this little detail that had me ask for a ghost whisperer. I never believed in them before.

That might have concluded our correspondence. But it did not. Here is what followed.

Hi, John,

Thank you for reading my emails. At my age, I find it ridiculous that I waited so long to piece things together. Since I wrote you last, I tried to remember other unexplained "episodes." Here is one from my early twenties.

Grandma passes away in October 1984. Of all my friends and relatives, including my parents, Grandma T. was the warmest person I knew.

In January 1984, both she and I had severe stomach pain and were diagnosed with gallstones. My doctor managed to remove my gall bladder right away, but I guess they didn't give my Grandma the same priority ... they just changed her diet. By June I was well recuperated, but when Grandma finally underwent the same surgery, her prognosis was poor. In her case, the gall bladder issue was not stones, but cancer, and her cancer had spread to most of her vital organs.

By the end of September, she was hospitalized and given weeks, if not days, to live. Mom and her sisters took turns sitting vigil by her side, until one October morning, when Mom got a call at about 3:30 a.m.

I took the call and Auntie asked me to inform my Mom that time was short for Grandma, and if Mom wanted to see her alive one last time and say her final "goodbye" she should rush to her bedside.

The hospital was minutes away. Mom refused my offer for a ride, but asked that I tend to our very yappy Pomeranian puppy and cat until she returned. There was no more sleep after that call, and I sat up thinking of all Grandma meant to me. Twenty minutes passed, and I found myself cursing Mom for not keeping her promise to call me when she reached the hospital. A few more minutes passed, when kitty started sniffing the air, sat upright, and just looked to the distance. Puppy started doing the same, but kept snapping at the air with her mouth, without making a sound, just a little whimper.

I was alone in the house, but not scared. Puppy usually made a stink whenever anyone climbed the front stairs and kitty always hid under the bed whenever someone stepped a foot into the house, so I didn't think much of their unusual actions.

No, I did not feel fear, but I did feel a very cold draft from my knees down. Grandma always told me to keep my feet warm, even though I liked the cold. The cold caught up with me, and no amount of blankets warmed me up. I estimate the time to be about 4:00 a.m.

Just after five, o'clock, Mom called to say Grandma passed at about 4:00 a.m. I guess our puppy and kitty were more aware than I was.

SHADOW PERSONS

Dave Nichols

It "makes my morning" to turn on my computer, check my email, and find a communication like the following one, which arrived on September 2, 2010.

> Mr. Colombo,
>
> I just finished reading your book the other day on true Canadian haunting stories. I am interested to know if you are still collecting stories of ghosts for your next book, as I have some unique experiences, such as seeing what people refer to as a "shadow person" and also having the sensation that some unseen presence was running their hands over my legs for a period of a few months. I also have other stories, but I feel these are the most unique, and I will send more along with these if you are interested. Thank you for your time.

I wanted to follow this up, as I have had men and women mention to me that they had felt the presence of "the shadow people" (in the plural) or "the shadow person" (in the singular). I wondered if this was another way of referring to ghosts or revenants. Perhaps it was a postmodern and up-to-date way of doing so, as the words "ghosts and spirits" and "discarnate entities" sound somewhat old-fashioned these days, as charming as that may be.

I wrote to Mr. Nichols and encouraged him to send me an account of his experiences. The following day, his second email arrived, accompanied by a long attachment.

Before I reproduce the account of the experience, here are some ideas that occurred to me. The words "the shadow people" are associated, at least in my mind, with the MIBs, the "men in black," the ominous-looking, black-suited, impassive-appearing men who seemed somehow connected with flying saucer and UFO appearances. They seemed to be secret service agents of some sort, perhaps even alien beings themselves. They were "shadowy." Mr. Nichols describes not these people so much as spectre-like, humanoid figures who haunt the hinterland between reality and darkness.

The first set of experiences occurred on Tolton Avenue in Hamilton, and the experiences in the second set occurred on Malibu Drive in Niagara Falls, both in Ontario. I am not sure what to make of any of this, and I suspect that you, the reader of this account, will be flummoxed as well. So I turn you over to Mr. Nichols's experiences....

Mr. Colombo,

I never had any experiences until I was twenty-six and living with my Dad in Hamilton in Ontario. I was living with my Dad in our one-storey house. We had lived there for five years without incident. I had a small interest in the paranormal from about the age of fourteen after my Mom had returned from a psychic and had played a tape from her reading, which was extremely accurate for someone that had never met our family.

I began to go on ghost walks with my then girlfriend after learning she also shared an interest in the paranormal. We had gone on about three ghost walks with a local company that offered guided tours, but with no encounters or experiences we were growing disappointed. We had booked a ghost walk for Niagara-on-the-Lake and in the fall about October or November, 2008. We arrived for the tour, expecting no encounters as with our previous outing and figured that it would just be a nice evening out.

It was when we were at the back of the tour trailing behind on a side road, staring into the darkened houses, that we both saw it — a blue light in the blackened building hovering about mid-level, and we watched as it crossed one window, disappeared inside the house behind the door, and re-emerged in front of the next window and made its way to the wall before disappearing completely. I immediately came to a stop and suspected one of the tour guides of playing a joke and would soon appear, as the guides were carrying lanterns, but no one appeared.

I began to look around for a logical explanation. First, the street lights were the normal colour. I peered around for headlights from cars but there were none. It must have been lights from the house across the street. As I looked around, I realized that there was only one house on the opposite side of the street, about one hundred feet away and no lights were on. Without saying a word, my girlfriend I rejoined the back of the group. I looked behind us, still expecting someone to emerge laughing and declare it was a joke, but no one ever came and all the tour guides were still at the front of the tour. I tried to forget it as something I had imagined, since my girlfriend had not said anything.

As the tour progressed, we stopped in front of a pharmacy while the tour guide was telling the story of the ghosts that were supposed to be haunting the pharmacy. I began to smell a strong scent of flowers. Puzzled, I looked around for an explanation. First, the large square bins that had lined the street and usually held flowers — there were none. A glance into the store for a display containing flowers — nothing. I was baffled that there were no flowers anywhere yet there was a sudden strong smell of flowers. I began to suspect that maybe one of the women in the group had some perfume with the scent of flowers, but no matter where I stood or who I stood next to, I never smelt the scent and my girl-friend made no mention of it. The tour ended and my girlfriend and I walked to the car. I was still thinking of everything I had seen and smelt and still had no word from her. I jumped into my car and opened the other door for my girlfriend. She got in and, to my shock, turned and asked if I saw the light in the house. I said yes and asked what colour it was. I asked it that way so that I would not influence what she had seen. Her reply was that it was blue, so then I knew I was not crazy after all.

My girlfriend then asked if I had smelled something in front of the pharmacy. I replied that I had but was unsure of what the smell was. She, of course, had said it smelt like flowers and I became more relieved that we had had the same experiences. Her next statement completely threw me off, as she had said that it was annoying her at the courthouse that I kept blowing on her neck while the tour guide was trying to tell the history of the place. I, of course, had not been blowing on her neck, as I was standing to the right of her and I am about eight inches taller than she is. She was quite sure it was, despite my reassurance it wasn't.

There were no other experiences in that house until the following year, in about May or June. I kept having a strong sense that someone was in the house, standing there, always in a different place in the living room, and looking around I always saw nothing, but the sense was so strong that I could have picked out exactly where the person was standing if I could only have seen them. Every couple of weeks, I would have the same feeling, always in the living room, but I never saw anyone or anything. In early December of that year, I was picking up my girlfriend on a Saturday and driving her back to my place, as was our routine. I drove in front of my house and noticed the house was in darkness. It was odd as it was about 8:00 p.m., and my Dad would usually have the lights on and begin to open the front door as he saw my car.

We pulled into the driveway and still no lights. I said aloud that it was odd. My Dad usually has the lights on. No sooner had I finished the sentence than the lights turned on, but the door did not budge. I turned to my girlfriend and made the comment that my Dad must be getting lazy, as he always opens the door when turning the lights on, and the door is about six inches from the light switch. We had exited the car at the stairs to the front door. I had opened the glass door, then turned the handle on the storm door, expecting it to open right up. The door did not budge — it was locked. Impossible, I thought, as I had seen the lights turn on.

I again tried the door with the same result — the door was locked. Just to be sure, I gave it a push and the door stood there in defiance and not moving. I was now concerned, as the lights had come on and my Dad would have heard me trying the door handle multiple times. I tried to stay calm and handed my girlfriend my cell phone and told her to stay on the porch and if I was not back in five minutes to call 911 and report that someone was in the house and I had gone in and not come back out.

I entered the house slowly and checked my Dad's room that was five feet from the front door. It was empty. I searched my bedroom and my Dad's bedroom and under beds and behind doors in closets. All were empty. Checking the living room and bathroom and kitchen still gave the same result. I returned to my girlfriend, who was still standing on the cold porch, and told her the main floor was empty and I was going to check the basement, knowing it was unlikely anyone went there. I approached the basement door — it was of course locked in place by the latch. Knowing that no one could have opened the basement door and latched it back in place from the other side, I slid the latch off and opened the door. The basement lights were off. I turned them on and went down about six stairs and peered into the unfinished basement. No one was in sight. The only possible hiding spot was behind the washer and dryer, and I took a quick look on both sides of each appliance and came up empty-handed.

I returned up the stairs, let my girlfriend in, and patiently waited for my Dad to return, as he was the only other possibly person that could have been in the house. About an hour approached before my Dad returned home. I jumped up and ran to ask him if he had been home about an hour ago and left as I came in the house. Of course, he was puzzled and replied no. I told him about the lights turning on, just as I said it was odd that they were not on. He simply shrugged it off and never spoke of it any more. I must admit it was a very late before I went to sleep that night. There were no further occurrences, and I moved out in July the following year to my Mom's house to become a volunteer fire fighter and figured that there would be no more experiences. I could not have been more wrong.

Moving into my Mom's house on the first day, I was tired and went to bed about 9:00 p.m. I had just finished turning off the lights and throwing a blanket over myself when it felt as if someone was rubbing my legs. I could feel fingers, but I thought that it was just the blanket near the air vent. The air conditioning was on and it had been blowing on the blanket and causing the sensation. I moved the blanket and it stopped for a second and then started again. I again moved the blanket and the same thing occurred. The invisible hands were touching my legs. I moved to a different location near the wall and still again it occurred. No matter how many times I moved or how I tried to sleep, the invisible hands still touched my legs. This occurred for about a month and then stopped just as suddenly as it had begun in August, and I was relieved as it was long nights before I got to sleep.

What happened next made me wish that the only disturbance to my sleep was the invisible hands. I was awakened one night by the thumping of the plastic piece on the blinds that you have to turn in order to open and close them. I looked and saw nothing but the blind turner bouncing in the moonlight against the blind. I tried to tell myself it was just the wind from the ceiling fan blowing it. Hours later I was finally able to sleep again. Then I heard the same sound of the blind, looking again as if it was bouncing off the blind, and yet no one was near it, and I was alone in my room, and for the previous month it had not done this once. For months, the blind turner would bounce off the blinds, usually waking me up between twelve and one in the morning.

Around October I began to hear a rustling noise in my closet on the garbage bags. Of course, I assumed that my cat had gotten into my room during the night and had made herself a bed out of the garbage bags of books and TV cables that I had not unpacked. I woke up in the morning and looked into the closet and found it was empty. But how had I not let the cat out, and upon thinking about it, my door was closed all night and I never let the cat in. Waiting until my sisters woke up, I asked if either one of them had let the cat in or out during the night and the expected response of no was given. I began locking my bedroom, so I was sure that no one was letting the cat in or out. The noise of the rustling garbage bags continued, but only in the night, and it always woke me up.

In December I decided to evict whatever animal had taken up residence in my closet. Early morning one day, I took out the three garbage bags and removed all the books. There were no rips or pieces torn off and everything was intact. But this was impossible. I thought, clearly, there was something living in my closet and I replaced all the items and returned the garbage bags to the closet, thinking it was all behind me now. That night, I was proven wrong, as the rustling continued.

Then, in January, I took the garbage bags out repeated the same process as before, and still everything was intact. My Mother slept over a few times a week when she worked, as she had to get up at 5:00 a.m. My sister that was the middle child and twenty-seven at the time would sleep in the living room.

One day in March, I awoke around 7:00 a.m. in desperate need of the bathroom. Getting up, I looked around the door through the kitchen and into the living room, where my sister had been sleeping. To my surprise, I saw a dark figure, which appeared to be my sister's. But she was in the chair, and her dog was not in her usual spot on the couch. I ducked back into my room, looked out again to be certain it was her and not my cat, which sometimes slept on the back of the chair. Nope. Definitely dark hair and my sister's shoulders. Ducking back into my room, I again looked out into the living room and decided it was my sister or my cat. Of course, I was certain it was my sister as I had now spent about three minutes staring at the back of her head and shoulders, and cats cannot sit upright in a la-z-boy chair. I threw on my pajamas and darted to the bathroom. I returned to my room, tried to sleep, but was still wide awake. I knew I should not have spent so much time seeing if it was her or not and just went to the bathroom.

I got up to go to make breakfast and talk to her, since we were the only ones awake. I went through the kitchen to the living room and got out the words "wow you're up early," and looking around the living room, I noticed my sister was not there. There was no sign of her at all, and most puzzling, the dog's chair she had been sitting in had clothes piled half-way up it. She is about six feet tall. She is a very tall girl, so if she had sat in that chair I would have seen more than just her head and shoulders. I went and got breakfast and sat waiting in my room for her at about 9:00 a.m., when she came out. I followed her into the kitchen and asked her why she had got up so early and then gone right back to bed in her room. She asked what time it was that I had seen her, as she had gone to bed around 5:00 a.m., when my Mom woke her up making her lunch for the day. I assured her it was around 7:00 a.m. and that I had seen her in the dog's chair, with her dark hair and shoulders. Her reply was that she has never sat in the dog's chair and she went to bed at 5:00 a.m. because it was still dark out when my Mom woke her up.

I got up the courage to ask her if she had experienced anything strange in the house. Questioning me as to what, I said was like someone touching you or like things moving on their own. She said, without any real thought or concern, that, yes, the spirits usually bother her when she tries to sleep in the living room, and she has a hard time sleeping in there, so she usually goes to her room as soon as my Mom goes to work. I inquired as to how these spirits bother her, and she said that they usually touch her or call her name.

I believe her, as I believe her to psychic as she claims and as she has demonstrated to me a few times. I was left knowing that I was not the only one with experiences in the house, and that I had seen what many people call a "shadow person." I do not have a better word for it, as it was a solid black figure with a head and neck and shoulders just like a person.

That night, I was in bed around one o'clock in the morning, when I heard the rustling of the garbage bag. My thought was the cat was in the room, and then I realized, of course, that she was not, and I sprung up from bed and reached for the light on the ceiling fan, expecting to see a mischievous animal that comes out at night like a raccoon or a rat that had gotten in. Nothing. Not even the bag was moving. Now, really annoyed as to all the lost sleep, I started to grab the garbage bags and pull them apart on my bed, in the middle of the night. I found nothing at all and no evidence that anything was in there or anything that had established any kind of residence. I was at a loss as to the noise. I put everything back and turned out the light and lay down again, only to hear the rustling of the garbage bags.

Waking up in the morning, I was still angry. I decided that I had to do something, but what? After seeing many shows on the paranormal on television and seeing the paranormal teams always advising their clients that they have to take back their home. You have to confront what is there and demand that they leave. I stood in my room and made an announcement that I had had enough, I was tired of all the noise from the blinds and the garbage bags, and I did not want any more disturbances, and whatever was there must stop or leave.

Going to bed that night, I was skeptical that anything would change. To my amazement, I slept without any noises. Whatever was here must have honoured my request for my beauty sleep. I have not had any more noises waking me up, and I have not seen any more "shadow people" in the last six months.

Spirits Will Never Harm You

Diana Noel

I received this email on September 19, 2009, and read it through with a smile on my face. Although it deals with odd events, as well as strange feelings, the correspondent writes with verve and high spirits. That accounts for the smile on my face. I am willing to bet there is a smile on her face too! (She sounds like a lively person.) Her name is Diana Noel, and I asked her for some biographical details to round out this account of peculiar occurrences in the house in which she and her husband and baby live ... perhaps with spirits! The account ends with the offer to share more experiences of strange occurrences. I naturally asked her to send them once she has the opportunity to recall them and write them down in detail. I think what the present account from Ms. Noel shows is that odd and peculiar things do occur ... right under our noses.

Hi there!

I was at the library last week, when I happened across your book! I've always loved the supernatural and paranormal occurrences and therefore enjoyed reading this book tremendously! I like that you invite readers to share their experiences with you. In this email, I shall share mine with you!

Since a very young age, I've always had "encounters" or "meetings" with supernatural beings. I haven't been spooked or met any evil ghosts that caused me harm in my meetings, but after each encounter, I have always thought long and hard and really enjoy "bumping" into them, be it day or night. I know it sounds crazy, but if you're like me, who hears "things" or sees "things" since a very young age (I'm now 31), you learn to embrace it. There's no point in being upset or overly worked up, as these entities usually do not harm you (at least the ones I have encountered!).

The story that I am sharing with you in this email happened about two months ago … and so I shall begin.

I hired a new babysitter, who came highly recommended by a good friend of mine (and I've met her many times before, too) to watch my four-year-old son for two hours while my husband and I went out for dinner. It was around 5:00 p.m. when we left, and I told the babysitter that we would be home, at the latest, by 7:00 p.m. So, I made supper (mash potatoes, chicken, and corn) for them, and as I usually tell all my babysitters, that she shouldn't worry about doing any dishes while we were gone and to just have dinner and then have a good time.

We came home half an hour earlier than expected, and when I was in the kitchen with her, I spied a frying pan in the dish rack, which wasn't there when I had left. I jokingly asked her if they didn't have enough to eat and that she had to make more food while I was gone. Her face went pale and she told me a strange thing had happened while she was sitting at the kitchen table with my son, eating supper. While they were eating, the frying pan suddenly came crashing down onto the floor.

I didn't think anything of it and went to check the hook that the frying pan is usually hanging from. It was fine. So I just hung the pan back onto the hook. I asked her if my son had cried when it had happened, but she said he just looked at the spot where the pan was hanging and calmly said, "Oh, oh," and continued eating as if nothing happened. Nothing else happened in my kitchen that day or the following week as well.

There was a night during that week when my husband and I went to the movies for three hours and I got her to babysit my son for me again. My son was already sleeping when I got her over, and she was sitting on the couch when we left. Everything was fine that night … or so I thought … until we were chatting the next time she babysat for me again, when I found out that her boy-friend had dropped by that night while we were gone. My rules for babysitters are: No smoking, no drinking, and no boyfriends. She broke a rule!

After that week, my good friend and I decided to go for breakfast in the morning and I thought nothing better than getting this same new babysitter yet again! (At this time I hadn't known about her boy-friend dropping by yet.) So I called her and got her to my house for 10:00 a.m. I had a wonderful time with my friend and came home around noon. I offered to make my babysitter a sandwich before she left, and so we chatted with her in the kitchen. She told me that she preferred to babysit during the day as she is free to play with my son, rather than watching TV. That's when she told me that her boyfriend came over the last time she babysat. Of course, I was furious, but I wanted to find out what else she did while I was gone that night, so I controlled my anger and kept on talking to her.

No, I didn't see any frying pan lying around, but what happened next is definitely an eye-opener. While I was cutting up some cheese, I sarcastically asked my babysitter, "So, no frying pan falling over today?"

She said no, and then, I don't know what possessed me to ask her, but I asked, "Hey ... do you believe in ghosts?"

She said no.

Then, I said to her, "You know, I believe in ghosts and spirits and things like that...."

At that particular moment, five kitchen lights (it's track-lighting) started flickering! Wow, I thought ... it's been a while! (When we had first moved into this house, three years ago, the lights in the foyer fre-quently flickered, and then one day it stopped flickering, and it has never flickered since.) My babysitter was so spooked that she asked me to send her home!

It was around noon, as I said, and the weather outside was sunny and beautiful. There couldn't have been a power outage at that time, and I believe it to be more than a coincidence, as I was explicitly referring to spirits in my conversations! Strangely, I didn't feel scared by this incident, maybe a little furious still at the fact that her boyfriend had dropped by while my husband and I were gone.

The very next day, though, I told my good friend about this incident, and I couldn't believe what she told me. She told me that this babysitter of mine is dating a boy, several years older than herself, and that his family disapproves of their relationship. What's even weirder is that this house that I am living in now — an older, beautiful-character home — was the home of her boyfriend's grandparents before the previous owners back in the 1950s. She thinks that it's the spirit of his grandparents showing their disapproval. I am not sure what to think, whether it's her boyfriend's grandparents' disapproval or my son's guardian angel warning me about her. I'm pretty sure that my son's guardian angel knows that I wouldn't be pleased at all with a babysitter's boyfriend dropping by at night while my son was sleeping and she's paid to babysit.

Whatever it was, I listened to the signs, thought about it, and never took her back as my babysitter again. Needless to say, there were no more crashing frying pans or flickering lights. I still do hear knockings and footsteps, but I am never afraid of them. I believe that if you've a good heart and good intentions, spirits will never harm you, as they've never harmed me!

I knew this house has "spirits" the moment I entered it. The first time I viewed this house with my husband and son, I felt it was a magnet drawing me to it! My husband needed a little convincing in the beginning, but he now prowls the house in darkness and nothing ever bothers him. (We like to conserve electricity whenever possible!) However, my good friend admits to feeling very strange whenever she's in my house, especially in particular spots. I don't though ... I often wonder why. Maybe the "spirits" of the house know me and my family by now. I'm not sure.

I hope you've enjoyed the story. I find it utterly fascinating and I definitely acknowledge that I had a brush with spirits that morning. To me, it's just a matter of when. I do not seek out spirits, but at the same time I am not afraid of them. As I am writing this now, I just caught a glimpse of something or someone at the corner of my left eye. Of course, it's just the doorway, when I fully look up.

I will send you some of my earlier sightings which occurred when I was younger, if you're interested! Thanks for your time!

I heard from my correspondent on September 21, 2009. She sent me the following response to my email, which consisted in the main of the above entry in this book. She responded positively to my request to write up her other odd experiences. Here is what she wrote:

What a busy weekend it's been for me and I definitely feel good knowing that you enjoyed my last spirit encounter! Some of the people I've recounted this story to had laughed and made jokes about it. It doesn't bother me one bit, actually. I guess that incident is one of those things that you have to be there to believe it! Having said that, it's always a pleasure to meet other open-minded people like you to share my stories with! I am down with a really bad cold right now, and will definitely share another story with you while I wait for my hot tea to cool....

This story that I shall relate to you is my first-ever encounter with a supernatural being. I was 13 at the time and had just moved into a brand-new house my parents had bought. One of the walls of my bedroom is adjacent to the living room. One night, my parents were having what seemed to me to be a very long conversation in the living room. There was no yelling or shouting, but I could tell that they were both upset over something. I had school the next day and this was around 9:30 p.m. (My bedtime was at 9:00 p.m., so I'm pretty sure my parents thought I was already asleep when they were having their serious conversation!) I kept tossing and turning and tried so hard to sleep but I just couldn't!

Anyway, as I was lying on my side, I suddenly felt a woman patting my back and saying, "It's okay, go to sleep." And she kept repeating it again and again. I felt all drowsy and good and so comforted when she did this. I say "a woman" because when she was doing this, it's a woman's voice I hear speaking to me. At the same time, I could hear my mother's voice fading in the background, yet every fiber in my being didn't scream with alarm at all! I felt very safe, warm, comforted, and secure!

The next morning, when my mother came into my room to wake me up for school, I asked her, "What were you and Daddy talking about last night?" She said, "Nothing." Of course, I knew they were having an argument, but I didn't tell her that! Then I asked her if she had come into my room last night. She looked surprised and said, "No." Then I told her what happened. She was surprised but maintained that she hadn't come into my room at all last night. My mother never talked about this "incident" with me again, but it certainly has stuck with me forever. My only theory is that my guardian angel had been there to put me to bed! Crazy as it may sound, why else would I have got what I wanted that night (to go to bed) and also be overcome with such warmth? I am still not sure who it was.

Referring back to my last story, where I speculated if it were spirits or guardian angels warning me about my babysitter, maybe it's the same entity that's still around after all these years. Who is this angel that protects me? Or even, who is this spirit attached to me all these time? I have been very blessed in my life in so many ways! It's something I would like to find out somewhere down the road.

I hope you enjoy my story. I am sorry if this email is a little short. My cold is getting worse as I'm typing to you! I shall send more stories when I'm all better. (Off to drink my hot lemon tea!)

Oh yes, before I forget: you may use my stories for your upcoming book. I am all for sharing my experiences! With so many questions I have about my encounters, maybe someday I may find my answers through my sharing! Glad you enjoy my stories!

GROWING UP WITH THE
SUPERNATURAL

Jeff P.

I received this long narrative account of "growing up with the supernatural" by email on August 6, 2010. It came from Jeff P., as he prefers to be known, a correspondent new to me. He wrote as follows:

> Hi, my name is Jeff. I have read some of your books and came across your email address and wanted to send you one of my own personal haunts. I have quite a few. So if interested then get back to me. If you like it and if you want more I have more to give.

Needless to say, I read his account and immediately emailed its author and asked him to send me more accounts, especially the one that refers to Niagara Falls. (For decades I have been collecting references to the Mighty Cataract.)

One detail in Jeff's story rings a bell. I grew up in Waterloo County and remember visits as a child to Puslinch Lake, which is near Kitchener, my hometown. Although I have not revisited the lake, or even thought about it in over fifty years, I retain the vivid feeling to this day that the place was and perhaps still is ... rather odd ... spooky ... unusual.

After reading these accounts, I now think it is ... unusual.

> It all started when I was just five years old. My father in all his wisdom had woken up my brother and myself to go and watch

some horror movies on TV. It was an old black-and-white one, by today's standards quite lame. But remember that this was back in 1976. (Yea, I am that old.) It had *Dracula*, *The Wolf Man*, *Frankenstein's Monster*, *The Mummy*, all the horror greats.

After watching those movies I went back to bed and had the first of my nightmares, ones that would plague me to this day, all the way to 2010. The nightmares would scare the hell out of me until the age of seven. That is when I had the first nightmare where I was the monster. It was great. It turned my fears around. Somewhat? Well, I still have nightmares today, every time I dream. But they don't affect me much anymore.

Now I know you are trying to figure out what all this has to do with the supernatural. I think it was the fear that brought me into believing in the supernatural. Well, when I was nine, my family moved out to Puslinch, into a very old farm house. It was known as the Walker Farm in Puslinch. It was not until July 2010 that I got some info on the property from the Puslinch Historical Society. I had found out that the property has been a farm since 1861, maybe even earlier. But, in one of the land surveys they had in their files, it states that it has been a farm since then. So that makes the house, the barn (where it all takes place), 149 years old. The first owners of the farm were the Maltby family. And before it was a farm or Puslinch was Puslinch, it was Indian land. And if you look up in the history of Puslinch, you will find out that there was a huge Indian slaughter there. You see, the Indians that were here first were farmers. And they were attacked by a warring tribe of Indians.

Again this is just the back story of where I grew up and had most of my supernatural events. Now I am nine years old, and it is 1980. My family had just moved onto this property in Puslinch. All seemed normal for a while. In the later part of the 1980s, my Dad had decided to renovate the farmhouse. My room was first, and when they were insulating my room upstairs, I had to sleep downstairs in the back room. Well, in the middle of the night, I had to get up to go for a pee and being half asleep and running on habit, I had walked upstairs to go to the bathroom, and when

I was done I came back downstairs. Instead of turning left to go to the back room, I went right, as if I was going to go to the TV room to watch TV, again being half asleep. Well, something white that looks like an arm went flying into my face. I woke up right away and ran to the back room and turned on all the lights and turned on my radio quite loud and hid under the covers. (Hey, as a kid we all knew that nothing could get you while you are under the covers.) Well, a few minutes later, down comes my Mom to yell at me for all the lights on and the radio playing so loud. I told her what I seen and she said that it was just my imagination and nothing else. (But she used much stronger words.) Even to this day, I still say it was because I was half asleep.

Now, the next thing that happened to me was when I was thirteen, so the year was 1984. It was around eight at night. My family and I were watching TV. My mother, father, and brother were all in the TV room watching, I think it was, *The Dukes of Hazard*. Well, it was a commercial and I went upstairs to get something in my room. Now, to get from the TV room to the stairs to go upstairs, there is only one pathway to take. (This is important information.) You would get up go through the TV room then into the kitchen then into the dining room. Then you are at the stairs, where if you go forward you end up in the back room. Well, I am leaving from upstairs, and as I was coming down the stairs, something made me stop and look up, and between the banister railings I could see right into my room and under my bed. When I looked in there, I saw a pair of socks come flying out from under my bed and hit me in the face. I took off like a shot and ran all the way back to the TV room, non-stop. My mother father and brother were still there. They had not moved since I had left. I told them what had happened and they made jokes about it. Well, I had to be forced to go to bed that night.

Also when I was thirteen, it was November, it was cold, and there was snow on the ground. My brother and I had adopted some barn cats. They came to the house one day, and we fed them and they came back and stayed around. Well, I was coming home from school and on the driveway was my cat. She had been run over. Well, I told my Dad, and when he got home he got rid of the dead cat in the basement yard of the barn. All was said and done. I was upset, but I knew there was no way to bring her back ... or so I thought. The next day, when I got up to go to school, there was my brother's cat and my cat back up at the house waiting for their morning treat. But my cat had died the previous day. I knew it was her because she answered to her name and she had a crease in her side where she had been run over. I told my parents and again they said it was a different cat. But later that week, my Dad gave all the barn cats away to a friend on a farm.

I was sixteen now, the year was 1987. My brother, who was eighteen, was off at his work, and so were my Mom and my Dad. I had come up with the bright idea of haunting the basement of the barn for Halloween for my friends and myself. I had just come home from school. I was alone and it was late September. Well, I went to go to the basement of the barn and, well, I got a weird feeling in the pit of my stomach. I had then decided to go back to the house and bring the family dog down with me. Now, she was just as freaked out as I was. I had to bribe her in with some cookies. She then came in with me to get the cookies.

Over the years my brother and I had fixed up one of the old horse stalls into a fort. (We never had any animals except dogs and cats.) The horse stall had two stone walls and two wooden walls. Now, the wooden walls went only half way up. So my brother and I, over the years, had filled in the rest to make it a complete room. My brother and I had hung a door on our makeshift fort. The only problem was, because we were not carpenters, the door would always swing open. Now, I put the family dog back in our fort on a blanket, where she was eating her cookies and watching me. I had wanted to go and get an axe to put in a post with a hat and some fake blood as a prop. Well, when I went to leave the barn, I looked into the fort and there was the family dog. So I told her I would be back and I closed the door and put a huge cinder block in front of the door to keep it closed. I left the barn, closed the outside barn door, went to the drive-in shed, and got an axe. I went back to the barn. The barn door was still closed. I opened it and walked in with a smile on my face and a whistle on my lips. (Life was good.) I went into the bowels of the barn where the fort was. Nothing had changed. The cinder block was still there. The door was closed and there was no way out of the fort. Well, I moved the cinder block and the door swung open. The dog was gone!

The first thing I had thought was that someone or something had taken my dog! I was now holding the axe like a weapon. Now, if it was my brother playing a joke on me, I was so wound up and freaked out, I would have hit him with the axe when he popped out. But no one was home except for me and the dog (wherever she was). I searched the bottom of the barn and then went up the stairs up to the top part of the barn, but still no dog. I was freaking out. My parents are going to kill me, is what I was thinking. Then something in my mind told me to look up at the house. So I did and when I went up there, the dog was there. I was so grateful that she was there and unharmed. After that time, she would not go into the barn at all, even for cookies or treats. And I did not enter the basement of the barn since then ... or a while.

I was now twenty-nine and the year was 2000. And true to my word, I have not been in the basement of the barn since 1987. But I had just bought a new digital camera with a flash. I wanted to try out the flash but did not want to wait till the night. I went back to the farm and entered the top part of the barn, went to the stairs to go down to the basement of the barn, and took the first picture. Now, when I took the pictures, I did not see anything unusual in them. But when I put them on my girlfriend's computer, I saw lots of things. I had taken about ten pics. (It was a cheap digital camera and I could not even upgrade the memory card on it.) So, in the first pic that I took I saw a face in the floor of the basement of the barn. It looked evil and mean. Well, that freaked me out a bit. Then I looked at the next few I took and one of them had some orbs in it. But, hey, it is an old barn and dirty, and when I took the flash pic the camera was aimed at a window on the other side of the barn. Then I looked at the pic that I took of the root cellar I had seen. Well, it looked like a lightning flash but there was no flash. It almost looked like a streak of ectoplasm. (I don't know what else to call it.) Then in another pic of a different root cellar, well there were two faces in the wall. And in the last horse stall, there was what looked like a giant human eye in the wall. Well, after I had seen those pics on my girlfriend's computer, I avoided the basement of the barn again for a few years. I had broken up with that girlfriend and never gotten the pics off her computer.

I was thirty-eight, the year was 2009. I had gotten in touch with a group of local amateur ghost hunters. They had heard my stories and wanted to check out the barn. So I took them into the barn. Remember, I had not been in the basement of the barn since 2000. My current girlfriend was with us. The ghost hunters had brought a psychic with them and the first thing that she had said to me was that my mother was standing beside me. None of them knew me and none of them knew that my Mom had passed away. So that was creepy. So, we went into the barn and the psychic told me that there are two spirits in the barn. One is of a little boy and one of his father, who was totally mean and very abusive while he was alive and even more abusive now that he was dead. This was a lot to take in. The group had taken pics and EVPs but came up with nothing. I invited them back to come to the barn one night to do an investigation. Again, they found nothing. (The psychic was not with them that time.) Again, she told me nothing or even showed me any of the pics that they had taken.

So, time went by and now I am thirty-nine and the year is 2010. (Yea, present time.) I had sent an email to a professional group of ghost hunters from Guelph. They came to the barn and the leader of the group, who also has some psychic abilities, said that as soon as she entered the property a feeling of depression overcame her. When we entered the top part of the barn, they started to take pics and filming with a camcorder. They were in the barn for only an hour but came out with a lot of proof. They even had done some EVPs in the basement of the barn and, wow, did they get lots of voices and growls and other unexplained noises. In the pictures that they took, there are a lot of orbs. Some are dust, yes, but some also have faces in the orbs as well as some glow. They had uploaded the images for me, so I do have proof and to those readers that had followed the story all the way through and want to see the pics, I will try to send them to the website that I have posted this story on.

Now, there are lots more things that I have done that involve the supernatural. But these are the only ones that happened to me where and while I grew up. I have other adventures in British Columbia and even Niagara Falls. If you want to hear them, I will type them up as well.

I continued to correspond with Jeff, and on August 20, 2010, he sent me what he calls "Part 3 of the Trilogy: Back to Puslinch." Here it is:

Well, we have come full circle here, dear readers. My trip through the supernatural, which first started in Puslinch, then took me to Niagara Falls. Now it comes full circle back to Puslinch.

The year is 2010, the month is January. I started a part-time job with a cleaning company. It was a job to help pay the rent. Well, one of the companies that we had to clean (my girlfriend and myself) was located in the heart of Puslinch. I am not sure why we had the problems that we had there. It was a new building, maybe no older than ten years. But when we had to go to clean the plant, it was the last on our list of companies that we had to clean. We would get there anytime between 11:00 p.m. and 1:00 a.m., and we would not get out of there until maybe 3:00 a.m.

When we got there, the first thing we had to do was to unlock the outer door, then the inner door, and then turn off the alarm. Then we had to turn on the lights and lock the front doors. So we were alone in the plant. We would go halfway through the building to get to where our janitor's closet was located. We would get our cleaning equipment, then we would part ways and both go around doing our cleaning. My partner would go into the bathrooms to clean them, while I would go to the back of the plant to start cleaning the offices.

But whenever would get into the back part of the plant, there was a feeling that someone was watching us. But there was no one there. (My partner and I were the only ones in the place.) Well, I would shove off the feeling and go around and do my work. I would see a shadow (possibly "shadow people") move out of the corner of my eye. It was a humanoid form, but when I would turn to look at it, it was gone. I would get the feeling of someone near me. I would hurry up and finish my work in the back area to get to the front of the plant.

While I was doing this, my partner was having problems of her own. When she would finish the bathroom, she would head up to the front of the plant to clean the front offices. There was a door that leads from the front offices to the research lab. Again, there was no one in any area of the plant. The alarm was on when we got there. The alarm covered the entire plant. Well, when she was near that door in the front, she would hear someone actually knock on the door. She would not answer it. (Neither would I, when it happened to me.) Well, she had said that once the knocking on the door started, it would get louder and louder, and then suddenly stop.

Meanwhile, I was leaving the back of the plant and working in the side offices in the middle of the place. I had heard a woman's voice say my name. (I thought it was my partner.) I would say, "Yes, what do you want?" No answer. I would say it again. Still no answer. Well, by this time I was getting a big aggravated. I would say the same to her, because I had heard her call me. After a bit of arguing, she would tell me that she did not call me. Then she would tell me about what happened up front to her. I would tell her what had happened to me in the back. We would switch tasks. I would finish up front and she would finish out back.

While I was up front, I did not hear the knock on the door but on the wall. That was the wall with the door. And while she was in the back of the plant, she saw the same "shadow" movement out of the corner of her eye.

One specific event happened only once in the plant. I was walking up from the back of the place and I saw my partner walking into a room in the front. I figured she was planning on scaring me. (I do it enough to her.) So I put down my vacuum and crept up along the wall up to the door which she had opened and entered. I jumped out in front of the door and yelled to scare her. But she was not there! She would come out of the bathroom behind me. Well, this went on for months. Then I kept seeing a woman enter one specific office. Every time we would show up, we would enter the same events. It was becoming a pain to go and clean this plant. But by this time I had left the cleaning business and had entered a new line of work.

Well, after I left the cleaning company, my partner stayed on with the cleaning company. I would ask her how it was cleaning the one plant in Puslinch. She would tell me that her new part- ner never felt anything weird around the building. Then my old partner's encounters started to get strange and more involved. She heard people talking when there was no one there. She said she saw an apparition of a woman who was wearing a period dress. The woman would look at my old partner and then go and walk into the staff lunch room. It has only one entrance and exit. My partner would get up some courage and go into the lunch room. There was never anyone there. Well, this was the last straw for her. She quit the cleaning company.

THE INCIDENT AT NIAGARA FALLS

You all know me by now with my haunted problems in Puslinch. Well, to continue with them, go back to when I am eighteen years old. I have moved out of my parent's house in Puslinch and moved to Niagara Falls. I lived in a youth hostel in the 'burbs of Niagara. I was in Niagara College and working part time at Louis Tussauds on Clifton Hill. The year was 1989. Louis Tussauds was located on the bottom of Clifton Hill, not where it is today. The history of the building that was Tussauds used to be the original Sky Fox Hotel. Now, when the Sky Fox moved out of their original building, they built their new huge hotel right beside the old one. Even the third floor of the original hotel was connected to the new Sky Fox Hotel. (They shared a wall.)

Well, getting back to the story. The building stayed empty not for long. It then became a religious museum. Then it became vacant until Louis Tussauds moved in. When it was vacant, it was a haven for bums and drifters to hang out in. And apparently some had died in there. I had just gotten a job with Tussauds as an assistant art director. Well, take the fancy title away from it. All I did was clean the wax figures in the museum. Within the first month there, I did my work during the day. I found out that a lot of the current people who used to work there noted that there was something funny about the museum. One worker had worked there for the past five years. She never once set foot in the museum after 3:00 p.m. When it was the hotel, on the second floor, when I worked there, there was the general manager's office. When it was the hotel, a woman committed suicide in that office. And I can tell from personal experience that something was still in that office. But I would not figure that out until they gave me my keys to do my cleaning at night. Now, about three general managers ago, they had one general manager die on the steps going up to the second floor. So there have been quite a few deaths in the building. (Maybe that is why it was haunted.)

Now, when I was doing my work during the day, I would have to take care of cleaning all the wax exhibits on the main floor and in the Horror Chamber. One day the art director asked me to go to the third floor to get some packing peanuts for her. I went up the old stairs to the third floor. (At the time it was just a floor that was used to store all their old wax figures and props.) As soon as I opened the door to the third floor, I got a very uneasy feeling that washed over me. I shrugged it off and started to go to the room where the packing peanuts were stored. As I was walking around, I swear that I heard footsteps behind me. I would call out, "Who is there?" but I would get no answer. I just figured that it was the art director or someone who was trying to scare me.

As I was getting the packing peanuts, I heard a phone ring. I stopped and started to look for the phone. I searched the entire third floor and could not find a phone anywhere. I gave up and went back down to the second floor and proceeded to give the peanuts to the art director. I told her about the phantom phone. She laughed at me and then told me that the third floor wall was attached to the new Sky Fox hotel. Then she asked me if I had heard the footsteps. I looked at her and figured that she was just making it up to scare me. She told me that every time she would go up there alone, she would hear the footsteps behind her as well. Then she told me some of the history of the building and about all the people who had died in the building. She also told me that they used to open up the Horror Chamber for Halloween to see if customers could spend more than one hour down there. If they could do it, they would give them passes to all the attractions on Clifton Hill. Let's just say that they did not have to give out any passes.

I shrugged it off and went down to the main floor and talked to a couple of the cashiers who were working there for some time. They told me that they got the creeps being in there at night and that they heard the footsteps on the third floor. Well, as time passed, I would do my work.

One day I was in the Horror Chamber doing some cleaning. Anyone who has ever been in the museum when it was on Clifton Hill, not above it where it is now, would remember the Horror Chamber and would remember that some of the wax heads they had in the wall. Well, to clean them, I had to go to the emergency exit and go through a side door, which leads me into a side room where they kept all the cleaning equipment. In there was a small door that was always locked. I had to unlock it and go through it and enter between the outer wall and the inner wall where they had the wax heads. Well, after one day, I was done cleaning in there and decided to go for a stroll. (Okay, I was nosey.) I followed the tight path and ended up finding a room that looked like it had once been used as a sleeping area for a hobo. In the room, I found newspapers from the 1930s, old rusty empty tins of food, and a lot of dust that had settled over everything. It looked like no one has been there for a lot of years. Well, when I was being nosey, I heard the footsteps again. I called out, "Who is there?" I saw nothing but heard the footsteps again. I got spooked and left quite quickly, meeting with no one. I locked the door again and left the Horror Chamber.

Well, I have now been given keys for the museum and was told to come in after they closed and do my cleaning then, so I would not disturb the customers. Good idea — not! My first mistake was to come in after they had closed down for the night and had gone home. So when I got there, I had to unlock the front door and enter the museum and then lock the door behind me. I had to find my way through the dark and then unlock another door. And in even more dark, I had to unlock a door to the main power room, then turn on the lights and take their CDs out and put in my own CDs so my own music played throughout the museum. Then I would go around the museum on the main floor. (By myself, I would not enter the Horror Chamber, especially at the night.) I would take off or turn around all the heads on the wax figures. (Hey, if I heard an "ouch," I was out of there in a flash.) Not many people know this, but the figure was wax only where the skin is seen, like the head and hands. The rest was a wooden, life-size doll. So, while doing this, I would pass the stairs to the Horror Camber and even with all the lights on (set lights and cleaning lights which were much brighter)I would not go down in. And again I heard the footsteps in the Horror Chamber.

Well, I decided to go up and clean the second-floor offices. I would get up there and a great feeling of sadness would come over me. I shrugged it off and would go to the end of the hall and clean my way back to the stairs. When I got into the general manager's office (the one where the woman committed suicide when it was a hotel room), the feeling of sadness would overcome me. I would start to cry for no reason, and then I would feel fear. Great fear. I would leave the general manager's office and make my way back to the stairs to go down to the main floor. I would get so frightened that I would end up cowering in a corner, shaking like a leaf. I must have passed out, because the next thing I knew it was 9:00 a.m. Oh, poop! I had to get the main floor of the museum cleaned up and the heads back on the wax figures and I had to turn their heads right around the proper way, all by 10:00 a.m. when the staff came in to start their day.

Well, this went on for about two weeks. I went through the same ritual and then decided that something had to be done. I told my one female friend at the time what was happening. She came up with an idea of how to cure me of the fright that I was having. (At the time it seemed like a good idea.) We went to the local flea market and bought a pair of metal handcuffs with keys. Well, she told me of an old abandoned house that was rumoured to be haunted. We showed up. The house was all boarded-up. We then removed one of the boards on the main-floor windows and entered and found an old radiator with some exposed pipes. She then took the handcuffs and attached the one half to the radiator and the other half to my arm. So I was chained to the radiator and could not leave. She then took the key with her and told me she would be back in one hour. The idea was that whatever was out there I had to face and could not run away from it. The next thing I knew, I was waking up in the back of her car. She told me that when she left the house she heard me scream and then came back in right away and found me out cold. She then undid the handcuffs and dragged me back to her car. Only a few minutes had passed. I do not remember what I had seen or heard. But let's just say that it did not cure me.

I had another idea. Why am I going into work at Louis Toussand's when they were closed? I decided to show up an hour before they closed for the night so I did not have to go into the building in the dark. That way I would have the security of knowing that people were in there with me at the time. At least for an hour.

I showed up to work and was confronted by one of the cashiers (there were two there at the time) and was told that in the Horror Chamber that one of the wax figures was broken. (This had been told to them by a customer.) Being that there were people there and the lights were on, I decided to go to the Horror Chamber and see what was wrong. In one of their exhibits it was of the rack and on the rack was a man (made of wax) that was being tortured by the other man (also made of wax), while on a pair of stairs that went nowhere there sat his wife (also made of wax) crying. Well, she was on the floor and her head and hands were smashed to pieces. Now, when wax breaks, it goes almost into dust. It is hard to pick it up. I went back up to the cashiers (they were both there) at the front of the Museum. I asked for the one cashier to come and give me a hand, so we could take the broken wax figure up to the art director's office to be fixed. Well, we both got down there and she was NOT broken! There were no signs that she was ever been broken. No wax dust or particles were to be seen. I knew it could not be a joke because we were the only ones there. And he could not have fixed the wax figure and cleaned up the mess it made and get back to the front of the Museum where I got him from. Well, that was the last straw, and I gave them my keys and quit on the spot. Thus ended my unexplained experience in Niagara Falls.

I Awoke to Find Myself Alone

Tanya Michelle P.

I am grateful to Michael J. Collee, who wrote to me to inquire if it would be of interest to me to read an account of some unusual experiences that occurred to his girlfriend on her family farm in Southern Ontario. I replied, "Yes," and I am pleased that I did, because a few days later I received this email written by his girlfriend, Tanya. She prefers to be identified as Tanya Michelle P. She has an unusual series of experiences to relate, and she writes about them with a great ease and even a sense of style. Her experiences are a delight to read. I notice that she is a student of English and Philosophy. (So was I!) Her email arrived on June 16, 2008. Here it is in its entirety. One or two of the experiences that she relates may or may not be readily explained, but as a group they beg the question: what is going on here? Read on....

Dear Mr. Colombo,

I am delighted to hear that you are interested in my paranormal experiences. I have thought about sending in my story for awhile, but my boyfriend, Michael, finally convinced me to do so. The incidents that I am about to recount to you all occurred on my family's 250-acre property, located outside of Simcoe, Ontario.

Before I begin, I would like to share a little bit of information about myself. I am a 22-year-old English and Philosophy student at the University of Guelph who plans to become a professor. I grew up as an only child in the rural "tobacco-belt" area of Ontario on a large farm, which is owned and operated by my family and has been for the last three generations. I experienced a fairly carefree childhood with no major emotional or mental ordeals.

I would like to begin by painting a picture of my farm, as it is divided into two sections and has many buildings scattered about it. The first section consists of two houses set back about 100 metres south of the road: a bungalow that my mother, father, and I reside in, and an old, two-storey farmhouse that has been abandoned for the last several years. There is also a large barn situated on the east side, behind our bungalow, and a small dwelling from the 1800s at the end of the main driveway, near the abandoned house. At the back, there is an older barn and a lone tobacco kiln. The second area of the farm, which is connected to the first area via a mile and a half long driveway through the fields, consists of a Victorian-era house and two older barns situated directly behind it. The house is currently occupied by my grandfather and uncle.

Strange Occurrences in the Old Farmhouse

The events that I am about to discuss took place on the first area of my property in the abandoned farmhouse. The farmhouse, which is constructed out of cinder blocks and consists of eleven rooms, was built in the 1930s on the foundation of the original house, which burnt down in the 1920s. I am not sure if anyone was killed in the fire, as my family had not yet emigrated from Hungary. However, in the 1930s, shortly after the current house had been built, a six-year-old girl died of pneumonia in the rear upstairs bedroom. My great grandparents then bought the house and property in the early 1940s after coming to Canada to escape the war. In the 1950s, my great grandparents decided to add a second kitchen and an indoor bathroom to the back of the house. However, during construction, the front step was upturned and discovered to be a child's headstone! My family is unable to remember the name on the headstone and has no explanation as to how or why the headstone came to rest in such an undignified place. Unfortunately, the headstone was misplaced and lost during construction.

In the 1980s, both of my great grandparents passed away in

the farmhouse. My great grandfather died first in the early '80s and then my great grandmother later passed in 1989. My uncle then moved into the house and stayed there from 1990 to 1999.

During the summer of 1997, my father, tired of the unreliable local farm help, decided to hire and house Trinidadian offshore workers in the farmhouse. This is when the strange occurrences started to be reported. After about a month of living in the farmhouse, the workers started to report instances of being strangled in the night by unseen hands. It got to the point where they would refuse to go in the house, choosing to sit and watch the sparse traffic on our road as opposed to watching a new colour television indoors. When forced inside by my skeptic father, the men would sleep with all of the downstairs lights on in the house and would often come to work the next day with very little rest. I remember seeing the look of pure terror on these men's faces. They were not joking. On the other hand, my uncle, who had lived with the men during the occurrences, said that he had not experienced anything unusual. However, my uncle, like my great grandparents before him, is a very hard-headed person who does not believe in the paranormal. Many of the offshore workers left at the end of the harvesting season, never to return. My uncle later left in late 1999 to live with my grandfather, who had recently become a widower. The house has sat unoccupied since, by anyone living anyway.

On Halloween of 2004, my friends and I had the grand idea to throw a small party in the downstairs living room of the old farmhouse. We invited about five people, wanting to keep the party limited to only our closest friends. The party consisted of no alcohol and everyone seemed in good spirits. During the night, while everybody was outside in the yard, I fell asleep on the couch in the living room. I awoke to find myself alone, and made my way through the original kitchen. I was fully awake when I heard a distinct hissing noise come from in front of one of the cupboards near me. I stood frozen, wondering what I had just heard. My first thoughts were that it was some kind of animal that had crawled its way into the cupboards. However, when I opened all of the cupboards, I discovered that they were all empty. Nevertheless, as

I sit and replay the experience back in my mind, I am entirely sure that the hissing had not even come from one of the cupboards, but from something unseen to me in front of it. Later that night, my friend, whom I will refer to as "Miss G.," awoke complaining of the feeling that she was being choked. I was very shocked by this as she had no prior knowledge of the choking incidents with the offshore workers.

In December of the same year, my friend, whom I will call "Miss C.," and I decided to place a video camera in the upstairs common area after she informed me that she felt a "presence" there. That night, both of us went into the house and set up the camera. I should also state that during this time, much of the wiring for the electricity in the house had become defective, so we had to do our entire set up in complete darkness. We were able to set up the camera fairly quickly by placing it on a pedestal ashtray. Suddenly, Miss C. became frightened for reasons unknown to me and took off running down the stairs to the front kitchen, leaving me alone upstairs. I then proceeded down the stairs but became held up by a random coat hanger that had found its way onto one of the stairs. I then met Miss C. downstairs and I shut the front kitchen door and we then both exited the house for the night. Both Miss C. and I returned the next morning to retrieve the camera and to play the tape on a large screen television monitor.

What we discovered on the tape made my friend leap up in enthusiasm and shout, "I told you so!" The tape showed that after Miss C. had left and I had cleared the hanger from the stairs and started to walk down, a large transparent orb shot out from the rear bedroom and started to go down the stairs that I had been on only seconds earlier. However, when I closed the door to the kitchen, the orb shot back up the stairs towards the same bedroom that it had exited from! It appeared as if the orb had been frightened by the sudden noise of the door closing. I am positive that it was not an insect of any sort, as it was the dead of winter and no creature could have survived in there. I am also positive that it was not an external light of any sort, as the orb appeared in places where there are no windows. The fact that the orb had both exited and entered the room where the little six-year-old girl had lived and died in sparked in me the idea that perhaps it was her spirit that was trapped in the farmhouse.

My suspicions became even more aroused the following January, when I discovered a fresh child's hand-print in the dust on top of one of the tables upstairs. I analyzed the very clear, tiny print which made my hands look enormous in comparison. I should also note that there had been no children on the farm and that it would have been impossible for a child to sneak into the house undetected, as the doors to the house were always locked tight. The only people who had been up in the farmhouse recently had been myself, Miss. G., Miss C., and my mother. All three other women have larger hands than I do, so it would have been impossible for one of them to have made the print. I asked each one of them as to the possible origin of the print, and all were just as baffled as I was. I then began to wonder if the child's headstone that had been recovered close to fifty years earlier could have possibly been the stone of the deceased young girl. Was she perhaps haunting the farmhouse out of anger? Later that same month, "Miss G." decided to take a few pictures of the downstairs of the house. Each picture she took showed clear and distinct orbs that were later determined not to be the result of a camera related error.

That following February, Miss C., Miss G., and I decided to spend a cold night (as the heating to the house no longer worked) in the old farmhouse just sitting around talking. We were sitting in the downstairs living room engulfed in deep conversation, when I began to hear what sounded like a dinner party coming from the back of the house. I kept it to myself, thinking that my mind was playing tricks on me. However, I found myself unable to concentrate on the conversation at hand between my two companions and me, as the clanging of plates and busy chatter started to grow louder and louder. Finally, Miss G. asked if anyone else was hearing what seemed to be a "busy festive gathering." Miss C. looked very astonished and commented that she had thought that she was the only one hearing it. Spooked by what we were hearing, we exited the house and did not enter it again for close to two years.

In May of 2007, my boyfriend, Michael, and his friend, whom I will refer to as "Mr. N.," persuaded Miss C. and me to again set up the video camera in the upstairs of the farmhouse. As before, the camera was taken up and left in the common area. The tape showed various wispy orbs, though none as intelligent as the one caught on video before. Also, light footsteps could be heard on the upstairs floorboards but with no visible explanation as to why. The most interesting point on the tape came near the end when the focus on the camera began to fluctuate for no apparent reason. It appeared as if a mist was in front of the camera making everything blurry. However, when Michael and Mr. N. returned in the middle of the night to retrieve the camera, the instant appearance of Michael's head coming up the stairs suddenly caused the camera to immediately snap back into focus. It was as clear as a bell. I am not entirely sure if this was a technical problem of some sort, but the strange way that the focus just seemed to snap at Michael's sudden presence is still rather fascinating. Michael is a trained student in cinematography and has worked with cameras professionally for years, and this sudden change in focus in the camera still baffles him to this day, as he has never experienced anything like it before.

STRANGE OCCURRENCES IN MY HOUSE

I have also encountered several unexplainable events in my own home (the bungalow situated on the first area of the property). I somehow feel that these events have a link to my grandmother, who died of cancer in October of 1999. I was very close to her, and was devastated when she passed.

When I was around the age of eight, my grandmother gave me a black watch that had a picture of Mickey Mouse (complete with moving arms to tell the time!) on the face. I loved the watch a great deal and wore it very often when I was younger. However, when I was eleven the battery died in the watch, so I tucked it away and unfortunately forgot about it. In July of 1999, my grandmother was diagnosed with terminal pancreas cancer and decided to live out her last days in the hospital. While in the hospital, my grandmother informed me that she wanted me to have her cherished seashell jewelry box. I later received the box and took it home and had it set up on my dresser.

I very much admired the jewelry box, both sentimentally and aesthetically, so I decided to transfer all of my jewelry into it. While I was transferring my jewelry, I came across my long-lost Mickey watch. I looked at it for a moment, observing that Mickey's hands were still stuck in the same spot as they had been the last time that I had come across the watch. I placed the watch in the seashell box and closed the lid. In the middle of October, about a week after my grandmother's death, I was digging in the box for a specific pair of earrings when I came across dear Mickey again. However, this time Mickey's hands were ticking and telling the time perfectly! I was very amazed and confused by this, as the watch had never done this before. I went to my mother and asked her if she had replaced the battery in the watch, but she replied that she had not. In fact, she said that she did not even know that I still owned the watch. The watch ran for about three months after this and then stopped working just as suddenly as it had started. I can never know for certain, but I feel that this may have been a sign from my grandmother telling me that she was okay. She knew that I had adored the watch, so it would have been a logical tool for her to communicate through. Mickey has not started up since and still resides in the seashell jewelry box.

A second incident, which terrified me, occurred the following September (about eleven months after my grandmother's death). I was home alone with my orange tabby, Harry, for the night, as my parents had gone to visit family. It was around eight-thirty in the evening and it was unusually dark outside for the time of year. I was sitting on the couch in the upstairs living room, feeling very upset because I had just had a very bitter argument with my mother. During the course of the argument, I had spoken some very rude and disrespectful things to my mother that I still regret to this day. Like me, my mother had been very close to my grandmother and spent almost every day with her on the farm. I know that my grandmother would have been very angry if she had heard the things that I had said to my mother.

Suddenly, as I was mulling the course of the argument over in my head, I heard a large crash come from my bedroom, at the back of the house. The crash was so loud that it sent Harry running as I sat frozen on the couch. My first thought was that someone had broken a window and was attempting to burglarize the house. I sat idle, waiting for any sounds of movement to come from my room, but there were none. I then collected my courage and proceeded through the kitchen and down the short hallway to my room. I flicked on the light switch and looked around my room. The window was secure and everything looked in order, until I discovered my favourite ceramic wall-hanging on the floor across the room!

I stood in a haze of confusion. The wall-hanging, which was of two orange cats and had been a gift from my grandmother when I was a child, had formerly hung in the entrance of my room. However, it was now over by my bed sitting face down. I looked up at the hook and noticed that it was still attached securely to the wall. I then picked up the picture and discovered that the hook on the back was also still firmly attached. I tried to rationalize how something like this could have happened, but I could come up with nothing. The wall hanging was not very heavy, so there was no way that it could have made such a large crash as it did, not to mention the fact that it also mysteriously ended up on the other side of the room. The only explanation that I can come up with was that my grandmother had, in some way, heard the conversation and was letting me know that my behaviour was unacceptable. My grandmother had not been a violent woman, but I think that throwing a picture that she had given me and that she knew I loved may have been her way of letting me know that I needed to clean up my act. I may sound over-sentimental, but it is not my intention. My house had no prior history of unexplained events until after the death of my grandmother.

It was also during this time that I began to hear footsteps going up and down the hallway and into my room. Now, this continued until I was sixteen years old and then suddenly stopped. I have not had any occurrences since. Not to read into things too much, but when my grandmother was alive, she always said to my mother and me that she at least wanted to live to see me turn sixteen. Unfortunately, she came up about three years short. The footsteps would always occur while I was in the downstairs living room in the basement. The hallway is directly above the living room, so it is very easy to hear when someone is walking up there. The footsteps were always of the same consistency (usually fairly light) and would usually occur when I was home alone. However, on one occasion both my mother and I heard them while we were in the basement. The footsteps were not those of anyone who lived in the house, as my father's footsteps were much heavier and my mother's footsteps were more hurried. Also, they could not have been my cat's footsteps, as all of these occurrences took place while he was outside. In addition, the footsteps were strictly limited to the hallway and there were never any sounds of anyone entering the house and walking through the kitchen to the hallway. The footsteps would walk up and down the hallway a few times and then enter my bedroom and stop. This occurred over a dozen times in the outlined time frame. I still have no earthly explanation for these occurrences.

STRANGE OCCURRENCES ON THE FARM

The outdoor fields and wooded areas of my farm have also been the site of numerous unexplained events. Two of the incidents that I am about to recount have become somewhat "legendary" within my family.

The first "legendary" incident involves my great grandfather and his faithful Clydesdale workhorse. It was a hot summer day in the 1950s, and my great-grandfather was out with his horse working the crops in the fields. He was in good spirits and had not consumed any alcohol or any other sort of intoxicating substance that could have explained what he witnessed that day. He was going about his business, when he looked up and suddenly witnessed the sky break open. It broke open to reveal what he described as "a small European town." He thought that he was hallucinating until his horse suddenly looked up at the sky and became completely startled by the vision. My great-grandfather's horse had always been reliable and had never acted out of turn before. My father recalls my great-grandfather saying that he could almost read the street signs the vision was so clear. Apparently, there were ladies dressed up, people walking in and out of small shops, and traffic bustling about the streets. Then, as suddenly as the vision had appeared, it receded into the sky and faded away. I've often wondered if this was some sort of breach in the spatial temporal continuum.

The second "legendary" incident occurred when my neighbour's brother was working a field that borders the northeast sector of my farm. I should also point out that in this area of my property there is an old cemetery, which dates back to 1830. The cemetery is virtually invisible today, as the stones have long fallen over and sunk into the earth. The incident occurred during the nighttime when the weather was clear and it was rather calm outside. My neighbour's brother was going about his work, when he suddenly spotted a woman dressed in 19th-century clothing and holding an old lantern. She walked along the edge of the wooded area where the old cemetery is located, all the while not seeming to notice him or the loud tractor. As I understand, she disappeared into the wooded area and was not seen again. Now, my neighbour's brother is a very serious and straight-laced man who is not easily scared. But this scared him to the point where he vowed to never again set foot on that area of land after sundown.

A third strange incident, which I experienced, was the sound of aboriginal music coming from the pine trees in front of my house. This incident occurred during a cloudless night in July of 2003. I was sleeping soundly with the window open (as I always do), when I was suddenly stirred from my sleep by the loud sound of drums being played. I arose from my bed and went to the window. There was nothing unusual in sight, but the music became clearer and more distinct. It was a very basic primitive beat of hand-played drums, much like that found in aboriginal songs. However, the strange thing is that it sounded as if it was coming from the pine trees right in front of me! Nevertheless, I looked even closer but could see nothing and nobody in sight. I should also mention that my farm is rather remote, so the likelihood of someone sitting in my front lawn with drums or a radio was highly unlikely. The music played for about two minutes and then suddenly stopped. I asked my mother and father the next morning if they had heard the music, but they said that they had not. I have not heard the music since.

However, on an interesting note, my farm recently had a spiritual water-witcher in to do some work on finding the old gravestones in the cemetery that I mentioned before. This individual is very gifted and is able to locate buried bodies and headstones by using a balance of her spiritual gift and her craft in water-witching. She located twenty-one bodies in the cemetery (most of which she felt to be those of women and children) and one possible intact headstone, which is soon going to be exhumed. She then decided to tour the property and to our surprise she discovered nine more bodies! Even more to my astonishment was the fact that she said the bodies were that of natives and that they are buried in the form of a sacred circle. The bodies are apparently on the first area of the farm near the back barn and kiln. I am not sure if this discovery has anything to do with why I may have heard the strange aboriginal music, but it sure is fascinating!

Prophetic Dream

Carrie Pierce

This next account comes from the spirited Carrie Pierce, whom you may recall from "Joanna I Think Her Name Is," on page 92. She explained that her Meadowvale Spookies Paranormal Research Team consists of a couple dozen members, who meet regularly and occasionally hold public events. These events are sometimes held at the Adamson-Grange House, part of the Mississauga Heritage Foundation. She was interested in having me speak there about ghosts and spirits, so she readily agreed that an hour's talk, titled "Toronto's Ghosts and How to Find Them," would have an immediate appeal.

This initial conversation took place in late September 2009, and on Saturday, October 23, between 2:00 p.m. and 4:00 p.m., I did just as we discussed — addressed an audience of the group's members and the general public who cared to attend. In the meantime, I wondered about Ms. Pierce, who seemed very lively indeed! It turned out she had a story to tell about her days in the U.S. Air Force, and I encouraged her to tell it to me in written words.

On October 2, 2009, I received the enclosed story by email, with a spirited account of her life and thoughts. I am reproducing all this here, with a little bit of reorganizing. What she describes is, in effect, a "crisis apparition." Although there was no apparition *per se*, phantom words were clearly heard, words conveying a message that the recipient had no easily explainable way of knowing.

I was born and raised in the small town of East Otto, New York. I had been exposed to the metaphysical and the paranormal at a very young age. My grandmother was an Italian woman who believed in mediumship and often took me to Lily Dale, until 1997, when I began a ten-year career with the United States Air Force. Being on active duty military did not stop me from exploring the paranormal. I involved myself with a few ghost-hunting groups during my tour of duty at the Langley Air Force Base, Virginia. Unfortunately in a military town, ghost-hunting groups come and go like the wind, because military people are "here today and gone tomorrow." While in Virginia, with my friends I explored some of the haunted historical sites in the district. These included two sites in Yorktown, Virginia: the famous Battlegrounds and the infamous Crawford Road. I also had the honour to assist in the investigation of a few residential cases.

In January 2005, I was assigned to Robins AFB, Georgia, where I was deployed to the Afghanistan region in support of Operation: Enduring Freedom. It was then that I had a life-changing experience, because of the ghostly phone call that I received in May of 2005. From that point on, I was driven to seek a deeper understanding of the supernatural.

I participated in a few groups in Georgia with the same "fly by night" status in Warner Robins, Georgia, another military town. But I also had the honour to befriend someone I call my "Paranormal Mentor," Andrew Caulder, a gentleman who is with the Georgia Paranormal Research Team out of Dublin, Georgia.

In July of 2007, I was honourably discharged from the U.S. Military. I am now settled with my husband Justin and our husky, "Diamond," in Mississauga, Ontario. I am striving to make the Meadowvale Spookies a strong-standing group in Ontario. I am on a "quest" — to seek other people who take paranormal research seriously. I like to say, "I run a tight ship, but I knows how to have fun too."

Here is what happened to me when I received that ghostly phone call in May of 2005.

I was working next to the mortuary and the bodies of two young marines were being held there, awaiting transport back to the States. They were kept in the caskets in the back of a van with a refrigerator box on it.

A day or so later, I got off my shift (I worked nights) and went to bed. We slept in these huge tents and there were, like, twelve women in one tent and each of us had her own section. There were tarps that separated each section for privacy. I brought my cell phone to use as my alarm clock because there weren't any alarm clocks over there at the base exchange.

I fell asleep and into a weird dream state. In this "dream," my phone rang and a faint voice with a smooth southern drawl said, "Hello? Pierce?"

I asked, "Who is this?"

It said, "Listen, this is Matt. You need to get up. Get your things together. You're packing out. There's no time get up now! This is your boy in the box."

After that I awoke, with my phone in my hand, as if I had been talking on it. I sat there awake. Not even twenty minutes went by, when my supervisor stormed into the tent and pulled my section-flap open, and told me to get up and get dressed.

Right behind her was the commander and the chaplain to give me the news that my father had passed away and I had less than one hour to get ready to leave.

Ironically enough, my dad was always a proud Vietnam veteran with the United States Marine Corps. That experience led me to develop a deeper understanding of the supernatural and the paranormal and made me desire to pass along what I had learned and to learn from others.

I Am Not Prone to Hallucinations

Barbara Piper

I received these emails from Barbara Piper on October 5, 2010. I have never met Ms. Piper, but after reading these accounts of anomalous events and experiences, I have a clear picture of who she is! She is sensitive, observant, considerate, and perhaps psychic. She is also family-oriented and straightforward. As well, she is a member of a close-knit family whose members experience psychic events, mainly connected with houses, their previous occupants, often at critical times in their lives and usually around falling asleep.

Abusive Man

I am 23 years old, never have nor ever will do drugs, and I am not prone to hallucinations. (I don't think I have ever had one, come to think of it.) The first incident took place when I was about 17. It was around June 2004, I think. I was staying at my boyfriend's house (now ex). I was sleeping in the guest room, which was on the main level of the house. (The house was in Embrun, Ontario, and as far as I can remember, was only maybe 30 or 60 at the most years old. I can't recall any mention of anyone dying in the house, but I never asked).

The room was set up like this: As you walked in through the door, there was a closet to your immediate right, and a smaller closet along the corner wall to your left. Across from you was a window, about 6 feet from the door. The bed was in the top right corner of the room, its head up against the wall to your right, and the foot of the bed facing the top left corner of the room. My first impressions of the room were mundane: it was a cozy room, with ugly wall paper. I didn't sense anything abnormal or creepy about the house or room before this incident.

Immediately to the right of the bed was a small table. On the night that this happened, I had not been drinking, and I was not feeling anything other than excitement about sleeping over at a boyfriend's house for the first time. I fell asleep rather quickly, and nothing disturbed my sleep until this happened. I wasn't completely awake, but I know for a fact I was not dreaming, either. I was conscious enough to know the direction I was facing (to the right) without opening my eyes, as I could "feel" that there was an object (the bed-side table) in front of my face. My first thought was, "What woke me up?" I had a distinct impression that somebody was lying down beside me on my left side, right behind me. I immediately thought it was my boyfriend, sneaking upstairs (his room was in the basement) to lie down beside me. As soon as that thought had gone through my head, I knew right away I was wrong, as I had a very strong feeling that whatever was behind me was evil.

I got the feeling that it was a man in his early forties who had been abusive towards his wife or daughter, and I looked enough like her that he wanted to abuse me too. I felt this "person" start to stroke my hair and then move their hand down my side, and continue down to my thighs, petting me. I knew that if I turned around to see who it was that I would regret it. I got the impression that they wanted me to acknowledge them. When I was little, I had the idea that if the monsters in your room thought you were asleep, then they would leave you alone (as they only bother children who are awake, apparently), so I would often pretend to be asleep so that they would leave me alone. (This was due to an over-active imagination, as I knew that there weren't any monsters in my room, but I was doing it as a precaution just in case I was wrong.) So this is exactly what I did. I pretended that I was asleep in the hopes that whoever was stroking my hair and side would go away. And it worked! I felt them get annoyed that I was not paying attention to them and I felt them leave. For some reason, as soon as they left, I fell asleep immediately.

I told my boyfriend what had happened, and he thought the house was haunted. But I never got that impression. I felt that this "abusive man" was in some way attached to the ground that the house had been built on. Not like a cemetery or anything, but maybe he had owned that land a long time ago, and the house had been built on his land. I never did any research on the property, so I am unable to verify any of these things that I felt.

IN THE BEDROOM

The next incident took place in my house, which is located in Osgoode, a small village just outside of Ottawa. For background info, my house is about 125 years old. To my knowledge, no one has died in the house, but then again, I never asked before. I have dug up many things in my backyard from the previous owners, as garbage pick-up was not a big thing then as it is now. I have everything from WWI pins, to a dime with the King on it from 1938 (made out of real silver), to glass baby bottles (the Even Flo ones), to plates and cups, and to many intact medicine bottles. I love archaeology, and I can spend hours outside digging in my backyard and the small woods behind my house.

So anyway, this event happened in my bedroom, sometime in December 2007. The way my room was laid out at the time was this: Upon entering the door, my bed was at the top right corner of the room, with the foot of the bed almost touching the door (if it is opened all the way; it is a small room, approximately ten feet by thirteen feet). I had a small bed-side table with a lamp right beside my bed on the left side. A window was right above the desk. I had (and have) pet rats, and Stanley's cage was right beside the desk, in between it and the closet. Lily's cage was across from Stanley's, right in front of my book case. (I had a bad habit of bringing home more pets than I had room for, so I had a hard time finding places for all the cages.) Right above my bed I had a poster in a heavy picture frame (I would guess five pounds, maybe) that was hung up on the wall by a secure thumbtack and had been hanging there for a year or two.

I was sleeping when I was wakened by a crashing sound. I reached over to turn on my lamp, only to find that it had fallen over, making the crashing sound. I picked my lamp back up and turned on the light to see what had happened. My first thought was that one of my cats had jumped on the desk, knocking over my lamp, but my door was firmly shut, and no cat was in my room. My window was closed tight, so it wasn't the curtains knocking it over with the breeze. I was perplexed. I also had a feeling that something was different in my room; something had changed, but I couldn't quite figure it out.

That's when I realized that the heavy poster above my bed was gone. I looked behind my bed (as that would have been the path it would have taken due to gravity), but it wasn't there. I looked over at my rats and discovered my poster lying unbroken, on the floor, in between the two cages. Somehow it flew across the room, knocking over my lamp, and rested on the floor. I was shocked, to say the least. I can tell you that upon realizing what had just happened, I was fully awake. I looked at the wall and saw that the thumbtack had been sheared off, probably from the weight of the poster. I looked over at the poster again and saw, rather alarmingly, that both my rats were staring at the empty space on the wall where my poster had been. I was getting scared at this point. I decided to leave my poster where it was so that I could show my parents what had happened. It was hard falling back to sleep after that, but somehow I managed.

In the morning, I told my parents what had happened, and showed them the broken thumbtack and where the poster was. Dad was of the opinion that I must have been sleepwalking and moved the poster for whatever reason. First of all, I have never sleepwalked in my life. Second of all, it would not have accounted for the broken thumbtack. And thirdly (and most importantly), it was the act of the poster knocking over my lamp that woke me up. If I had been the one moving the poster, then when the noise woke me up, I would have been holding the poster in my hands, not getting up from under my covers. The lamp would have been knocked over first, then the poster placed down, not the other way around. I thought about it for a few days and couldn't come up with anything other than a small feeling that what had taken place had been a guarding spirit protecting me from a heavy poster that could have fallen on my head.

I have also had other small things happen, like always seeing something small and black move out of the corner of my eye, but I have never seen anything when I look directly at it. (A very small number of these sightings could be explained by a mouse running across the floor, since we live in the country and do have mice living in the walls of our house.) I can recall sometime in the spring, several years ago, of having been wakened up one night with the distinct impression that I had just been tucked in. I mumbled a "thank you" and went right back to sleep. I know it wasn't my parents, as they have not tucked me in since I was six, and this happened when I was, I guess, fourteen or fifteen.

I have also, just recently (like, maybe three months ago), wakened myself up talking in my sleep. I remember saying something like "Ok, bye" to a man who had been talking to me. I don't remember what he was saying other than "I have to leave now." I am pretty sure this was not a dream, as I had nothing visual with it. I always have quite vivid dreams, usually about the woods in my backyard having abandoned or dilapidated houses in it, or of a small one-level house being haunted by my great-grandmother on my mom's side (I never met my great-grandparents, as the last one died shortly after my parents were married, so a year before I was born). I always remember my dreams in great detail, right down to the colour of clothes, or intense feelings.

OCCUPIED COAT ROOM

Another incident I had was with another ex. (Strangely enough, I haven't had anything happen with my current boyfriend, other than a strong sense that he is my soulmate.) It was around Easter, 2009. I was sleeping over at his parents' house. His mother had died of cancer when he was twelve, so I never met her, and at the time of the incident, I hadn't see a picture of her, so I didn't know what she looked like. Anyway, my (ex)boyfriend and I were lying in bed, trying to fall asleep, when I suddenly got the feeling that somebody had walked into his room. I "knew" it was his mom coming in to check me out. Then she walked out of his room after seeing who was with her son. I "felt" that she had long, slightly curly, dark hair. It turned out that before she had chemo, she had dark, wavy hair. (She was Italian.)

Also, in that house in the basement (his room was there, too), was a small coat room. I got the very distinct impression that a man was inhabiting that room and that he was quite angry at people who kept going into his space. I got the feeling that he was attached to the property, that he had a house on that spot before my ex's house was built there, and that the coat room was basically in the same spot as either the man's bedroom, or the spot where he died (maybe both). I hated going into that room. I started to whisper (so that my ex's stepmom wouldn't hear me, as she would have thought me completely nuts!) to the man, "I'm sorry that I have to come in to your space, but I just have to get something. I will be out in a few minutes. I'm really sorry about the others, but they don't know you are here." Whenever I did that, the feeling of hostility and anger was lessened anytime I had to go into that room.

GRANDPARENTS' HOUSE

This story takes place in the house that my granny and grandpa used to live in. It's in Ottawa, close to the Glebe. The way the house was set up was like this: Walking through the front door, there was a long hallway directly in front of you that ended in the kitchen. To left of the hallway was the stairs. The only bathroom was located at the top of the stairs. (You had to be really careful when opening the door to make sure you didn't knock anyone who might be in front of it down the stairs.) To the right was my grandparents' bedroom. Standing in front of the bedroom (with its door way to your left) was another hallway, ending in a small room that my granny used as her computer room. To the left of this room was a spare bedroom where we kids would sleep. At the bottom of the stairs (on the ground floor), with the front door on your right, was the living room, with the dining room at the end of it. There was also a doorway at the left of the dining room that led directly to the basement, on the left (which was also directly under the stairs), and the kitchen, to the right. Sorry if this is confusing.

The story goes that a long time ago (like when they used leather for book covers, and you had to shovel coal into a furnace), before my granny and grandpa lived in the house, it was owned by a doctor and his wife (or she may have been the landlady, and he was just a tenant; we are unclear on this one). This story was told to me and my younger brothers by our grandpa. He loved to tell us fantastic stories about ghosts and ancient buried treasure. (He also liked to blame his flatulence on the swans by the river, so we could never quite figure out if his stories were true or not.) Grandpa said that the doctor guy's room was in the basement. (This has always been odd to me, as the basement is one giant room, with no bathroom, and it is all rough stone walls and floor; very cold, and smells like moth balls.) The lady's room was on the top floor. He said that one day, the doctor guy just disappeared. He left his books, his fold-out chair, and his medical bag. He just left. I have no idea how long the lady lived there after this, or if an investigation ever took place into the guy's disappearance.

My grandparents bought the house sometime in the '50s. Grandpa said that he had to shovel all the coal out of the basement. (From the way grandpa described it, I am under the impression that the coal was right up to the bottom step of the stairs, kinda like if it was flooded; not sure if this is accurate, as all I know is what he had told me.) While shoveling the coal out, he came across the leather-covered books, which he promptly threw out as they were rotting. He also found an old fold-out chair, and an old leather bag, the kind a doctor back in those days would have carried.

He also said that he found a rock sticking out of the floor of the basement. He described the rock as being like that of a headstone. (Grandpa liked to embellish things for us kids. He loved telling us about seeing gremlins on his British war plane during WWII. I am not sure if this stone thing is real, or just something he added to the story to make it more cool.) He said that he was unable to dig it out, so he just snapped it off at its base. (For whatever reason I never asked him to show me the spot in basement where he broke the rock.) Grandpa said that he never had any issues with the house until he broke that stone. After that, strange things would happen. He went on to say that every once in a while, you would smell this really strong floral perfume come out of nowhere, then disappear. No one in the house (my grandpa, granny, my dad, his brother, or his sisters) wore perfume like that.

My dad used to tell me that their dog, Boots, used to sit in front of the front door because it was nice and cool. Every once in a while, Boots would get up, all the hairs on his back would be standing on end, and he would start to growl in the direction of the basement. No one could figure out why. My dad also told me that one night when he was nine, I think, he was sleeping in the room (later used as my granny's computer room) with his brother, when he turned over in his sleep and briefly woke up. He said that what he saw scared him so much that he screamed! He said that standing beside his bed was a man dressed in old-fashioned clothes, bent over my dad, just staring at him. He said that man was black and white (like from the movies) and was thin like cardboard. The man was just staring at him with wide-open eyes. My dad hid under the covers and screamed.

He tells me that he has had many strange dreams (or possibly hallucinations) while growing up in that house. Of the many dreams (or hallucinations) that I can remember are (in no particular order, as I have no idea when they occurred) of him seeing a cloud of bugs, worms, and maggots hovering over the crib of his baby sister; masks chasing him down the hall after using the bathroom; seeing seagulls on the wall of his bedroom; seeing a slow-motion, instant replay of a football player making a catch; and of seeing two astronauts in full gear pointing at him and apparently discussing my dad. My dad has no explanation for these events, and chalks them up to bad cheese and an over-active imagination.

My brother has stated that one time when he was sleeping over at my granny and grandpa's house (sleeping in the spare bedroom), he saw a face hovering on the wall by the night light. (I am pretty sure this is what he said. I can get back to you on this when my brother comes home from work.) I had never experienced anything in the house, other than a distinct feeling of not being alone when I was trying to sleep. And I was always nervous about the closet in the spare bedroom, and I would always sleep with my back to it. (It wasn't really a proper closet either. Just a carved-out space in the wall with a curtain over its doorway.)

My aunts can attest to the fact that they never liked being in that house alone. My dad even gets nightmares about the house. He says that he dreams he is inside the house and something or someone wants him to leave. He knows he has to get out, and so he runs for the door. He runs as fast as he can but the door keeps getting farther away, and the "thing" is closing in on him. Just as he is about to get to the door (or just as the "thing" is about to reach him, I can't be sure of which), he will wake up.

The house is no longer there in the same capacity as it was when my grandparents owned it. After my grandpa died from skin cancer, my granny sold the house. It has since then been torn down and rebuilt. Incidentally, I felt the presence of my grandpa at his funeral. I was with my (ex)boyfriend at the time (the one whose house that "abusive spirit" was in), and we were nearing the end of my grandpa's funeral service, when we both looked at each other and said, "He is here!" I could feel him "envelope" me. I know he was just saying goodbye. I didn't get any impression of any feelings (either happy, sad, or having unfinished business), nor did I get any messages from him. I just felt him around me.

GRANNY AND THE "UFO"

As for my granny's UFO story, I will have to see if dad has a copy. If he does, I will ask to borrow it and I will copy it out for you. My granny also has had a ghostly encounter. It happened shortly after her father died. She was staying with her mother. (I'm pretty sure granny was at her mother's place.) Granny was sleeping on the couch when she was wakened up by a bright light and a buzzing sound. It was coming from a corner of the room, near the ceiling. She said it looked like a sparkler (like one of those candle things that you can't blow out), and the buzzing sound was growing in intensity, as was the brightness. She said she knew it was her dad, and he had come back because he wanted to take her mom with him. Granny told her "dad" that it was not her mom's time to go yet, and that he had to go back. I can't remember how long this lasted, but eventually Granny persuaded him to leave, and I think the light and buzzing sound just faded away. Granny was a little frightened, but I think she was more frightened over him wanting to take her mother than what had just happened. Also, I think this incident happened a couple of days after he died, or after the funeral, not sure which. I'm not sure if this took place in Ottawa, as I have never thought to ask where her mom lived.

GHOSTLY EXPERIENCES

There have also been ghostly experiences on my mom's side, too. I think mom once told me about a time when her grandfather died, and he appeared to his wife (my great-grandma) to tell her that he was okay, and that she didn't need to worry about him. My great-grandma might have talked a little bit with him, I'm not sure. But I know it didn't last for very long, and it only happened once, that I know of. I'm pretty sure this happened in Massachusetts.

My mom once saw the ghost of her cat. Her cat Toby had died about two days before. He was a striped tabby cat. She was young, between nine and ten. She was walking in the kitchen when she saw out of the corner of her eye, her cat Toby sitting on the buffet cabinet. She described him as being like a mist or fog, very wavy, but she knew it was him because not only was it a cat shape but she could see his stripes. I think she said she looked at him for a couple of seconds, and when she blinked he was gone. This incident took place in North Gower, I believe, during the late sixties. (Mom was not on drugs, nor had she been drinking at the time, as she was probably only 9 or 10 years old.)

EVIL CADILLAC

I can remember one summer when I was about thirteen (so about 2000), my mom and dad were looking around for a new car. There was a used-car lot near our home, so they went to have a look. I can remember coming home from somewhere and seeing this Cadillac in our driveway. My parents said that the car was one of the ones they were looking at. They asked me if I wanted to go for a test-ride. I hopped in the back.

I hated it. I felt this evil presence with the car, like someone or something did not want us driving "their" car. It was overwhelming to the point that I flatly refused to get back in that car. I even told my parents that if they bought it, I would never ride in it. It was evil. They ended up going with another car, thankfully. I can still, to this day, feel the hatred that presence had towards us being in "their" car. I knew that if we bought it there would have been an accident.

DÉJÀ-VU AND ASTRAL PROJECTION

I can't think of any more stories at the moment, though I am sure I am forgetting one or two. If I remember, I will send you an email, hopefully along with my granny's UFO account. I suppose you need background info on me (for mailing me the book if my story appears in it, as I have read you do). My name is Barbara Piper and I was born July, 1987. I was born and raised in Ottawa until we moved to our current house in Osgoode, shortly after my fourth birthday. As I stated before, I have never done drugs, I never drink enough to get drunk (none of these things happened during a time when I would drink, anyway), and I have never had hallucinations, nor have I ever been known to sleepwalk. I have had strange feelings of people behind me for a long time. And I get very strong déjà-vus. Sometimes I have a déjà-vu that I have had a déjà-vu of this very moment (so, in effect, a double déjà-vu). I have never seen or heard a spirit (at least not when awake), but I can certainly feel them. And sometimes at night, when I am trying to sleep, I can feel myself "leaving my body," what people call astral projection. I try not to let it happen, as it is not something I practise, and I am never sure if I will be able to get back into my body.

I remember one night (I can't recall what month or year, sorry) I was trying to sleep, and I felt myself leaving my body. I don't know how high I was, but I get the sense that I was in another level of being, not quite space, but not quite on earth either. I was getting scared because I didn't want this, and I had no idea how to get back into my body. I called out (by thinking the words in my head) to anyone who was around me to please help, as I was inexperienced and I didn't know how to get back. Almost instantaneously, after crying out for help, I was back in my body. Even just recently (last week, in fact) I could feel myself starting to leave my body. I just concentrate on staying "inside," and I am able to fall asleep without any problems.

The Town's Name is Atikokan

Barry Roberts

I like the sound of that: "The town's name is Atikokan." I also like the sound of "Atikokan," which is the Ojibwa word for "caribou bones." The community is now known as "the canoeing capital of Canada," but in the past it was renowned for its iron ore and its forest products.

Strange things are recorded as happening in Atikokan, including the famous Steep Rock Sighting of a UFO in the 1950s. Readers with a copy of my book *UFOs over Canada* may read about that peculiar story. It is a vivid account of how a flying saucer landed near a lake and robot-like alien beings stepped out of it, organizing a refuelling of the saucer, which then took off. It is vivid all right, but the account was an elaborate hoax that was taken seriously by the news media of the day.

All of this was brought to mind by this letter from Barry Roberts, a reader of my books who grew up in Atikokan but now lives in Hamilton, Ontario. His handwritten letter arrived on July 7, 2009, forwarded by Dundurn, one of my publishers. In the letter, he asks if there are such things as daylight dreams. There certainly are. We dream while asleep, and there is ample evidence that at odd times we catch ourselves dreaming while awake. Daydreams may be as vivid as nightmares. Mr. Roberts also asks if butterflies fly by night. I believe they do!

Here is Mr. Roberts's letter *in toto*.

The Town's Name is Atikokan

Dear Mr. Colombo,

First, I'd like to thank you for all your excellent books. I am now reading the many stories of your *Big Book of Canadian Ghost Stories*. As you're on the lookout for new stories for new books, I thought I'd drop a line or three and tell you some of the strange things I've seen over the course of 52 years.

I come from a small town in Northern Ontario. Originally a mining town of 14,000, it is now a tourist town of 2,000. The town's name is Atikokan. It made it into a UFO book when a miner said he saw a UFO land on Steep Rock Lake and it took water from it. As he watched, little figures could be seen in the windows. It then sped away — true — the UFO book believed it — but the miner claimed he made it up as a laugh.

As for my experiences, the night skies back home were very clear, so it was always nice to sit outside in the summer time. My mom and sister would join me. Many nights we would see lights in the night sky, small lights, performing stunts that planes could not do. When I was around 14, I was sitting on my front porch, when I noticed something in the distance. It was some kind of ship (UFO?). It was immense in size, so I ran into the house to find the small telescope I had, but the ship was gone by then. Maybe it was a blimp, but why would a blimp be flying over a town in the middle of nowhere?

A question for you: is it possible to have a waking dream? When we lived in Thunder Bay for a year (Grade 5), I read the book *Legend of Sleepy Hollow*. Later that night, I woke for some reason and looked out the window. And there, walking on the telephone wires, was the Hessian, horse and all. It scared the crap out of me, so I ran downstairs and looked out the front room window. Still there. Went and hid under my mom's bed after that.

Speaking of my mom, she told me that when she was younger, she saw a very bright something above the farm. This was before the advent of jets and helicopters. It was right and loud enough to frighten the farm animals.

Later on, when we had moved to Toronto, this was in my twenties, I had an experience that was very strange, strange, but one that was seen by my brother-in-law Rob as well as myself. My mom was living by herself in some apartment near the Moss Park Armoury on Queen Street East. Rob and I had just finished bringing a couch to my mom's place and were on our way home. We pushed the button for the elevator. It came up, the door opened, and for a split second I saw a man dressed head-to-toe in black, just as he stepped to the side, as a person would, to let other people on. But when we entered the elevator, no one was there.

I asked Rob if he had seen the man also. He said yes he had. What would it be? A ghost? Omen?

Later, when I moved to Hamilton, the strangest things that happened were upon the roof of the building, where I've worked for 22 years as well as lived. One night I was up on the roof, getting away from the heat of the building, when as a joke I said out loud, "Give me a sign." And out of nowhere a meteor appeared with a tail around a mile long.

I said the same thing later, and a monarch butterfly flew by my face. Strange, because it was around 3:00 in the morning. Do butterflies fly at night?

THE FEELING OF BEING WATCHED

John Rochon

I always enjoy checking my email, because I receive communications from the readers of my books. Many a reader will write to share events and experiences of their own with me and with my future readers.

Such is the case with John Rochon, a reader who lives in Sarnia, Ontario, who sent me this email, which I opened on June 29, 2009.

Dear Mr. Colombo:

I recently read your *Big Book of Canadian Ghost Stories* and found it fascinating! It's rather comforting to know that these experiences are more common than one would imagine.

Reading your book got me to thinking about my own strange experiences, which have been occurring for as long as I can remember. I was raised in a "haunted house," then when my family moved from that house, we found ourselves living in another "haunted house"!

The attached story is about life in the second house, in which I resided less than two years. I have also worked in places where strange things happened, and continue to do so.

If you find the attached story interesting and would like stories about life in the first house, just let me know and I'd be happy to compose them for you.

Intrigued with Mr. Rochon's well-written letter, I immediately opened the attachment, where he describes, in some detail, "the sense of being watched." Psychologists have noted this phenomenon, as have researchers and writers who have contributed to the literature of paranormal experiences. Do human beings possess "a sixth sense" that permits us to sense the presence of personalities or powers that are unseen? The sensation is sometimes called "the entity experience," whereby our bodies seem to respond to energies or intelligences that are non-human or not fully "there." My own sense of it is that we have more than five senses (indeed, psychologists often state that there are nine human senses, including the sense of balance) and that some people are much more sensitive than others. In the nineteenth century, another name for a medium was a *sensitive*. So I believe we often sense things that cannot be seen, like odours and perhaps emotions generated by pheromones. Certainly places, both familiar and unfamiliar, have personalities all their own. Perhaps auras are really pheromones. Perhaps there are "pheromone personalities" — people who give off distinct personality traits or people whose senses are such that they can detect them.

Early in 1985, my family moved from the house we had resided in since October of 1963. Our "new" house was located on Cameron Street. It was a small, old, two-bedroom, one-storey house with a basement.

Having been unable to complete the move in one day, I volunteered to stay in the house alone overnight, while the rest of my family prepared to complete the move the next day at our old house.

Since none of the furniture had been brought over, I camped out on the living room floor. All through the night I heard footsteps and had the strong sensation of being watched. This sensation was strongest in, of all places, the bathroom! I had little sleep that night.

The next day we completed our move and set about the business of settling in. It wasn't long before other family members and friends also felt that they were being watched in the house. The house, which is on the south side of the street, had a central hall that ran through the house from the front door to the kitchen in the rear.

Off of the hall on the east side were the two bedrooms, the front bedroom which was occupied by my two brothers, and the second bedroom which was occupied by my parents. Behind their bedroom was the kitchen, pantry, and stairway down to the basement.

On the west side of the hall was the "parlour," followed by the living room, followed by the bathroom. Since there were only two bedrooms and five of us, I slept on a sofa bed in the parlour. The sofa bed was a very cheap one, which I had purchased earlier in anticipation of renting my first house, which eventually fell through. While lying on this "bed," I could feel the tread of anyone walking down the hall through the pressure on the floorboards.

One night while I was laying in "bed," not able to sleep, I felt and heard someone walk down the hall and stop at the front door. Thinking this to be my father, who was in the habit of getting up in the night, I rolled over to look out at the front door and found no one there. At that precise moment, my parents' bedroom door opened and out came my father!

It was not uncommon to feel a presence in the basement, and quite common to hear footsteps upstairs while in the basement and alone in the house. What disturbed me the most was the feeling of being watched in the bathroom, particularly while in the shower. The bathtub had an enclosure with sliding frosted-glass doors, but this in no way alleviated the feeling of being watched. In fact, at times it felt as if someone was actually in the shower with you!

We had three cats at the time, and these poor creatures were tormented time and again. They would often sit and stare at things unseen, or would jump up in the air from a dead sleep and rush out of the room.

I moved out of the house in the fall of 1986, but my family remained there until after my mother's death in 1997. The house has since been remodeled inside, drastically changing the interior

layout. I wonder if the presence still wanders the house at night —
I guess I'll never know.

Here is a second account of an eerie experience from
John Rochon, who lives in Sarnia, Ontario. It is so fluently
and neatly written that the reader is bound to be carried
along reading it. The account arrived by email on August 3,
2009.

What we have here is an early childhood memory that, for
close to four decades, has been supported by and interpreted
as a family tradition. Rather than ridicule young John when
he describes what happened to him, members of his family
have sought to reconcile him to what he had experienced. It
became a family tradition that "just George" was responsible
for the eerie encounter or experience. This is a "memorate"
if there ever was one! I expect memories of such experiences
are more common than we realize. Mr. Rochon's is certainly
vividly recalled.

THE HOUSE ON MARIA STREET, OR "JUST GEORGE"

I was born in the summer of 1963. At that time, my family (mom,
dad, sister, and brother) lived in a small house near Russell Street.
This house is believed to be the oldest house in that area. The larger
house immediately west of it was originally a local plumbers' shop,
which was converted into a residence in the mid-1950s. These
two houses are connected by a roof spanning the four-foot space
between them. Therefore, they are considered a duplex.

The owner of the duplex, George, resided in the larger house
on the west side with his family, and I believe that his was the first
family to reside there. George passed away in the house in 1961
or 1962, and after my birth an arrangement was made with his
widow to "swap" houses, affording our growing family with the
extra room we so desperately needed.

Even though our new home was larger, it had only two bedrooms, one on the main floor and one at the west end of the second. At the top of the stairs was a wide-open space with the attic running down the south (or rear) of the house, and a narrow hall with closets running along the north (or front) of the house between the two dormer windows. This space was utilized as a third "bedroom," using a bunk bed.

The first ghostly experience that I can recall occurred when I was about five or six years old. My sister, who was the eldest child and the only girl, had the bedroom upstairs, while my brother occupied the space at the top of the stairs. One night as I lay sleepless on my stomach, looking at the light from the streetlight outside that was shining in through the dormer window, someone unseen ran their hand up and down my spine, then grasped my right shoulder briefly. I know there was no physical being there, as the head and left side of my bed were both set against walls, and the right side and foot were plainly visible in the light from outside. I recall being frightened, however, but not enough to wake my sister or disturb my parents. When I related my experience to my mother the next day, she told me not to worry about it, that it was "just George."

From then on, whenever anything unexplainable happened, which was often, it was not as frightening, because it was "just George."

Experiment with a Ouija Board

Bernie Sardo

A continuing puzzle has been the operation of the Ouija board. In the 1940s and 1950s, one of these boards was commonly found in every closet in every home where there were young children. The Ouija board was brought out for use on rainy weekends.

For readers who may be unfamiliar with this device, which is also known as a "witch-board," it was (and is) manufactured and sold solely for the purpose of amusement, not divination. But it was always felt to have divinatory powers. At the time, Ouija boards were routinely denounced by ministers and priests in pulpits of churches, but that did not stop good little Christian boys or girls from using them.

The Ouija board is simply a yellow-coloured, shiny board with black characters on it. In a semi-circle, the letters of the alphabet are arranged, the numbers from 0 to 10, and in two of the four corners the words YES and NO are placed. A combination of the French and German words for yes (*oui, ja*), the board was not complete without its planchette, which was usually heart-shaped. This was a tiny platform that rested on three felt-tipped legs. It took two people to operate the planchette, ideally one of each gender, each of whom would lightly rest the tips of the fingers of one hand on the planchette. Then the operators would solemnly promise not to consciously move it around the board to spell out a message or the answer to a question.

Then someone would ask a question that went, "O Ouija ... ?" After a short pause, the planchette would begin to move around the board, slowly at first, then rapidly, with its tip pointing to YES and NO, or letters, or numbers that seemed to answer the questions that were solemnly asked. The operators of the board swore that they had not consciously moved the planchette. Psychologists would explain the planchette's action as "ideo-motor response," that is, involuntarily willed action: "the idea is father to the thought." In other words, the participants were willing to direct its movements without realizing they were doing so. No youngsters believed the psychologists with their rational explanations. The effect of spirit-directed propulsion is overpowering and quite surprising.

I received the following email on April 15, 2008. The reader is invited to make of Mr. Sardo's experience what he or she will. From my childhood and youthful experiences with "the board," I am able to testify that his account is psychologically accurate and that it catches the atmosphere of a session with an "active board." Sometimes the board "does not work," and it is lifeless and useless. When it does work, it seems, almost, to be ... "the work of the devil."

I subsequently queried Mr. Sardo for further details. He replied, "I've enclosed a few additional bits of info. My frightening experience occurred around 7 years ago, sometime around January or February 2001. Me and my friend did not tell anyone about our experience up until this very day. I have preferred not to include my phone number or postal code. I don't really want the attention. However, I have been in contact with my friend, and he does not mind if you use his real name in your book. His name is Mark Kovacs. Other than that, I can't remember anything else that happened, other than that I was afraid of the dark for a very long time after my experience."

To Mr. Colombo,

I'm reading your book *Strange But True*, and it's very interesting. Currently, I'm about halfway done it. I have a little story of my own to relate to you. When I was 10 years old, my friend and I decided to experiment with a Ouija board. We were looking for some thrills, so we decided to try and summon up a spirit, preferably an evil one. As we asked the board to bring forth a ghost, the planchette slowly moved towards the word *Yes*. We asked if the spirit was a male, and it stayed on the *Yes*. I thought that my friend, whose fingers also rested on the planchette, was slowly manipulating it to creep me out. I asked him to take his fingers off it, which he did. I took my fingers off it, too. Next, we asked if the spirit was good or evil. To our shock and horror, it spelled "E-V-I-L." By this time, we were both scared out of our wits. In a frightened voice, my friend asked out loud, "How many of you are there?" And, quite audibly, an evil voice whispered, "*Legion*." Crazy with fear, we both ran up out of the basement where we were holding our little seance. It was around one-thirty in the morning, so we both sprinted upstairs, into my friend's room, and quickly locked the door. We both stayed awake until morning. Ever since then, I've been warning others not to mess around with Ouija boards. They aren't a game.

My Experiences
in the Haunted House

Lauralee Shehirian

"Dear Mr. Colombo," wrote my correspondent. "Here is the account of my experiences in the haunted house. If you have any questions please feel free to ask. Please let me know what you think and if you find any more information about this house. Thank you." The email, which I read on August 22, 2008, was signed, "Lauralee Shehirian." In an earlier exchange of emails, I learned that the events described below occurred in 2003–04 in the farmhouse on Highway 35/115 just outside Newcastle, Ontario.

There are many features of this account that I admire, including the cast of vividly drawn characters, the sense of time passing, the feeling that these events and experiences defy rational explanation, yet the overall sense of rationality and humanity. I particularly like Ms. Shehirian's statement, "It started to dawn on me that the strange things that were happening were perhaps more than just coincidences." (This sounds like the long-suffering "Mrs. Miniver," who was played by Greer Garson in the 1942 Second World War movie of that name!) Mrs. Miniver knew she had to cope. Ms. Shehirian knew that too. Her record of these events is all the stronger for that sense that life has to go on, despite the distractions, setbacks, and (yes) the frightful events that took place ... that seem to continue to take place ... in that place of the poltergeist.

When we first thought about moving to the farmhouse on the 115, it seemed like such a good idea. My two kids and I needed a place to stay, having just left my soon to be ex-husband. A trusted friend and his partner offered to move into this house with us, and help us pay the rent. It was big enough for all of us, and either we moved there, or my kids and I would have to go to a shelter. We were told that it was haunted, but I didn't believe the ghost stories about it. Yes, we were shown an article that described a horrible crime that happened there, about a man who slaughtered his family in the house, burning his little girls alive and murdering his wife, then hanging himself in the barn. But what would that have to do with us, renting the house decades after the fact? If I knew then what I know now, we would have went to the shelter.

Several strange events began happening shortly after we moved in. They were little things that were easily explained away or rationalized at first. Lights in the house were constantly flickering, and at times I felt a cold wind in areas that had no airflow or reason for drafts. Other times I felt sudden cold chills. My computer would act strangely also. It would be off and then all of a sudden start playing the same song over and over again. The song it was playing even had those words in it: "Over and over again." I wasn't alone in seeing these strange events. My son, Brennan, heard strange noises in the night, coming from his closet, where there was a door to the attic. It seemed easily explained away as just animals or bugs, or that the house was just old and creaky.

People living in the area acted strangely when we told them where we lived. It was as if everyone knew something about that house, but no one wanted to talk about it. When pressed, we were told that it was haunted. It seemed that everyone knew about the murders that happened there. We started to do some more research, and there were numerous articles online about it. Brennan had to take a taxi to school on occasion, and the driver warned him to be careful around Halloween, but didn't elaborate any further as to why he would warn him so. He did tell Brennan a story about a girl that ran out of the woods near the house onto the highway, and was struck and killed by a truck. She was never identified, and no one in the area was missing. No one knew who this girl was or where she came from, why she was in the woods, or why she ran out in front of the truck.

It started to dawn on me that the strange things that were happening were perhaps more than just coincidences. My daughter Kristen complained that cups she placed on the kitchen table kept disappearing and would reappear five minutes later. She thought at first that I was playing games with her, hiding the cups and then returning them when she wasn't looking. But no one was in the kitchen when it happened, and I certainly didn't move the cups around. Things seemed eerie, but still I didn't want to succumb to a belief in haunted houses. I started to see lights and shadows moving about from under the bathroom door. There was the sound of little children's voices late at night, when everyone was asleep. There was no explanation for it. I started to worry.

The night that I really started to worry was when Brennan was sleeping and was woken to the sound of the fan in his room, turning constantly and bumping into the wall. The power had gone out, and it was strange that after the power came back, the fan started to turn, when it had been set to stay still. It had also pushed his alarm clock to the floor, where it fell and landed upside down. The power had come back on before Brennan woke up, and he saw the clock blinking the time. But instead of the expected 12:00 flashing when the power goes out, the clock was blinking 11:34. The clock being upside down, it read: "hell." The time didn't advance and stayed that way for quite some time, and it was very unsettling for both Brennan and myself, when he told me about it. I started to worry that something was in the house with us.

Another day, Brennan had come home from school to find an "X" carved onto his bedroom door. No one had been home since he left for school in the morning, and no one knew how it got there. Brennan had also told me he had heard a knocking at the front door on the second floor. There was indeed a door at the front of the house on the second floor, who knows why one had been built there in the first place, but there was no way someone could be knocking at it from the outside. Another day, he was out 4-wheeling in the field, when he came near to the barn, and it suddenly shut down without warning. He thought he heard someone running in the barn, and when he looked he saw the shape of a man running around inside. He assumed it was one of the two people living in the house with us at the time, but when he came into the house, I was sitting with that person in the kitchen. When he went back to take another look, the sound had stopped and no one was inside the barn. No one had gone in or out in the short time that Brennan came in to see us, and we never knew what had happened that day. His 4-wheeler was in good working order and there was no explanation as to why it shut down at that spot. The barn itself was creepy: the noose which the murderer used to hang himself was still there, undisturbed for decades, as if no one would dare to cut it down or remove it.

Kristen had a friend come over for a visit one day, and she was taking her picture, when the wall behind her friend suddenly turned pink while looking through the camera. Nothing else turned pink, not the bed or the furniture as would be expected if the camera was malfunctioning. It was just the wall and nothing else. Scared, they ran out of the room. After summoning up the courage, they returned to the room, where everything seemed normal. They did not attempt to take another picture there. Brennan had another strange experience while taking a picture of the house. There on the second floor, in the window to my room, there was someone's face in the window. He thought it was one of the housemates, but neither of them was home. In fact, no one was home at the time, and the face was unable to be discerned. The picture was lost sometime afterwards, and couldn't be found.

One night, at a friend's insistence, we played with a Ouija board. Kristen, my friend, and I were startled when the board repeatedly went back and forth, spelling out my son's name. I felt as if someone or something was trying to tell us something, and I was further convinced that the house was in fact haunted. Kristen had heard some more accounts from local residents of strange events at the house. She was told of a lady who had lived there with a baby, and always heard a baby crying, but it wasn't her child. She also heard another story of an eye doctor's family who lived there. After numerous strange events and inexplicable occurrences, they reportedly heard gunshots, and all ran out of the house, never to return even to collect their belongings.

We had with us two dogs at the time. One day, when I was alone, the dogs started to bark aggressively from outside, as if there was someone in the room with me that they didn't like. They were going crazy, as if trying to warn or protect me from someone they sensed next to me.

I felt ready to leave the house myself, and in fact had already begun looking for another place to stay. Towards the end of our time there, I was out in the backyard with my kids and our friend, when I saw a woman walk by us in the back yard. She didn't stop to acknowledge us or say anything; she simply walked out of the woods and past us towards the driveway. When I followed her, she was gone and there was no trace of her. No one else had seen her at all. When we were finally leaving the house, I was in the car with Brennan (Kristen having already left earlier) and we both heard and saw the car door open and close, and although no one came in, we both distinctly felt the presence of someone else in the car. This presence did not frighten me however, as most of the other occurrences had. I simply felt the presence of someone in the car, with no sense of evil or maliciousness. We drove away from the house and I hoped never to experience another strange event there. But I have always felt drawn to the house, and still frequently drive past it on the highway.

The strange events continued, however, even as time moved on. I remarried, and still drive past that stretch of highway with my new husband frequently. We both have seen strange things as we drive past. For example, one night as we drove past, after weeks of seeing no lights at all, and a FOR LEASE sign in the window, lights were on in the second floor, coloured lights that were not the normal lighting for those rooms. With no one living in the house, this was puzzling indeed. Also on the barn is a rather large advertising poster. This has a light that is always on so it can be seen from the highway.

One night we happened to be driving past at exactly midnight, and the light went off, precisely at midnight. We have driven past it before on many occasions, after midnight, and the light is always on. It seemed strange that on that night, exactly at midnight as we drove past it, the light went off, as if it was reacting to our driving past it.

But the most creepy thing happened only a few weeks ago, as we drove past the house at night, and there were two people standing under a light at the rear of the house, next to a side door. This door did not have a light, but there that night there was a light above the door. Both my husband and I saw different things. I saw a little boy and a teenage boy with him. My husband saw a little girl with long hair and a woman, who was most likely her mom. They didn't move, and simply stood, facing away from the highway, apparently not doing anything other than just standing there. We both looked at the same thing, but saw completely different things. Both of us were completely sure of what it was that we saw, and each of us was confident about our own account of what was there.

After living in the house for a number of years, and hearing the stories we heard about it, I became convinced that the house is in fact haunted. We tried to research it further recently, but nothing about it remains online, as if someone had gone and hunted down every article about it and had it deleted. It still gives me chills as we drive past it, and I can feel myself drawn to it, as if something wants me to go there. I can't explain any of it, but I'm glad to be free of it before anything further happened.

I Told Them Her Name Was Ena

Ronda Tanfield

This account was sent to me by Ronda Tanfield, who writes very clearly and very well about a very interesting subject. That subject is what psychologists know as the notion of the *Imaginary Playmate*.

Ms. Tanfield herself uses the words "imaginary friend," so she knows quite well that a childhood may be enriched by a short periods during which a child engages in harmless play "with someone who is not really there." Children are seldom able to distinguish between what is and what could be. There is much literature on this subject, both psychological and imaginative. But there is also a fair amount of literature on the subject with a supernatural twist: when the description of the unexpected friend or playmate corresponds in many particulars with the description of someone, usually another child, who has just died or who has a history of appearing to other people too. That is somewhat disconcerting!

The account here is one of exceptional clarity. I have no doubt that Ms. Tanfield has recalled her experiences in depth and recounted them with great, almost painful honesty. I do not know what to make of her experiences, but over the years they have enhanced rather than diminished her appreciation of life and its mysteries. In fact, they may have turned her attention to aura and Tarot reading and other New Age activities.

Dear Mr. Colombo,

I have enjoyed reading three of your books recently: *Ghost Stories of Ontario, True Canadian Ghost Stories*, and *True Canadian Haunting Stories*. I don't know if you are still looking for stories for any upcoming publications or not, but here is my story. If you can use it in any way, please feel free to do so.

My name is Ronda Tanfield. I was born in Weston, Ontario, in 1958. Several times a year, as a young child, my mother and I used to visit my maternal grandmother, great-grandparents, and great uncle (brother of my grandmother), who lived together in a small bungalow at 1392 Kenmuir Avenue in what was then Port Credit.

As you can imagine, there wasn't much to do for a young child with all those older adults around, but I used to look forward to those visits, because there was always a young girl there who was happy to see me and was very eager to play with me while the adults had their tea and talked. I always envied her long ringlets and pretty face and enjoyed her company, though her dress was very old-fashioned and she wore thick stockings. She told me her name was Ena and she always seemed fascinated by the toys that I would bring to play with, as if she had never seen anything quite like them before.

My mother was curious about my play behaviour during those visits as I sat all afternoon chatting quietly away to my imaginary friend, something I never did at home. (I was an only child until I was eight.) During one visit, my mother and grandmother asked me whom I was playing with. I told them the little girl that is always waiting for me when we arrive. They asked me if she had a name. I told them her name was Ena. My grandmother told me years later that a shiver went right down her spine. She asked me what Ena looked like. I described her ringlets, pretty face, and long dress like the one my Raggedy Ann wore. I was incredulous that "the adults" couldn't see her!

Years later, when I was in my late teens, my grandmother asked me if I remembered playing with Ena as a child. Of course I did! My grandmother then told me who Ena was. Back in 1918, my grandmother, her six siblings, and their parents were living on a farm in rural Haliburton, Ontario. Their home was under quarantine because the dreaded Spanish Flu pandemic of 1918 had reared its ugly head in their home and several of the children were terribly ill. Unfortunately, little four-year-old Ena succumbed to the illness, the only fatality of the family. The other children eventually recovered. My distraught great-grandparents were terribly upset that, due to the quarantine, no church service, proper burial, or any contact with the community was allowed. My grandmother told me that Ena was laid in the back kitchen while my great-grandfather took apart some wooden crates and fashioned a rather rustic coffin for poor Ena. He waited until the middle of the night, and with the help of a neighbour (whose family was also under quarantine) they stole into the night with their small box and buried Ena near the fence of the church cemetery.

I had never heard this story; it was a family secret that was never spoken of. I had no idea that my grandmother had another sister. She asked me if Ena seemed real to me, like a real solid child, or rather a transparent ghostly apparition, or just a spirit that I talked to in my mind. Ena was a real, solid person; all the years that I played with her she was a real person to me; there was never anything "ghostly" about her. I did wonder though, as I grew older, why Ena didn't seem to get any bigger. She didn't seem to age the way I was; she always seemed to be four years old and the same size.

I was stunned to learn that Ena was not a real child that I had been playing with all those years. I tried to remember the last time I played with Ena, and I really can't quite remember how old I was at the time, probably when I became too old to be bringing toys to play with on our annual visit. I do remember, when I was eight years old, being scolded for making too much noise in my play because my great-uncle was napping. Ena and I were running around the house playing hide'n seek, squealing and giggling.

It makes sense to me that if Ena's spirit was going to be any-where, it would be with her family, living with her sister, brother, and mother (my great-grandfather died when I was six or seven), living in that house in Port Credit. I'm not sure why Ena chose me as a playmate. When my sister was born in 1966 and the visits continued, she never saw Ena.

Ena does seem to have some kind of attachment to me for some reason, though. I enjoy taking night classes at the local schools; I am now living in rural Meaford, Ontario, and have enjoyed classes in Tarot card reading, aroma therapy, emergency pet care, etc.

It was in 2005 that I took a night class in aura reading at a school in Owen Sound. About a half hour into the class, the instructor, whom I had never met before, midway through her talk asked me who the child was that was hovering over my shoulder. I looked around because I was sure she was talking to the person behind me. No, it was me. She asked if I had lost a child. I replied no, that I had never had children of my own, but that my sister had lost a child. No, she was adamant, this was definitely a child of mine and that she was right at my shoulder. As I have said, I have never had children of my own, nor have I had a miscarriage. Who could this child be? My only explanation is that it must, for some reason, be Ena. Since we had so much fun as children, has Ena attached herself to me for life, perhaps as my guardian angel?

Of course, my great-grandmother, grandmother, great uncle, and all of Ena's other siblings are gone now, so if it is Ena, it gives me comfort to know that she is still with me after all these years and that she hasn't been forgotten.

I Was Absolutely Stunned

Lorraine S. Waller

I received the following email on May 20, 2010. It is rich in description of place, personality, and feeling.

Dear John:

I want to thank you once again for printing my story in *The Big Book of Canadian Hauntings*. I have never in my life been so thrilled.

Here, following, is yet another true story, one that happened to me in June 2008, while in hospital for three days. It takes place in Guelph, Ontario, where I reside.

Please feel free to include it in your next book, and I hope to someday meet you.

The email set me thinking, and I recalled that Ms. Waller had submitted a story, which I had accepted for that 2009 publication. I had given it the title "The Unmistakable Brightness of His Eyes." The story described, with stark terror, the informant's vision of a phantom child in the kitchen of the family's new home:

I opened the fridge to pour myself a cold glass of ice water, and as I shut the fridge door, I came face-to-face with a boy hovering about 3 feet in the air. Never in my entire life have I been so shocked. I remember I gasped, and my mouth must have been agape.

He appeared to be around 14 or 15 years of age — with big blue eyes, and blonde curly hair. I still do not understand to this day, why I did not drop my glass, but I was all at once astonished, but also thrilled that I knew I was finally viewing my very first apparition.

From it, I concluded that Ms. Waller was somewhat psychic and that she enjoyed ready access to feelings and sensation. Not many people do, for most people are defensive and guarded, fearing social ridicule with exposure.

I always encourage "experiencers" (if I may use that term) to keep in touch. I have found that people seldom have a single anomalous experience in a lifetime; instead, they have multiple anomalous experiences over the course of a lifetime. It seems such experiences are characteristic of people rather than places, and that they often run in families.

Here is Ms. Waller's account, one vivid in descriptions of the inner life following the experience of death.

My dearly beloved mother had passed away in February of that year, 2008. I was devastated. My life-force was nearly crushed out of me. Her thirteen-year battle with breast cancer made her finally succumb, and she died in the Orangeville hospital. My four children and I barely knew how to cope, let alone get through the experience day-after-day.

The level of my health started to decline. I was full of remorse, guilt, and regret. I could not find closure, and I felt that my heart had been ripped out of me. There were many times when I thought I would die from grief.

Three months went by, and my health plummeted. It was one thing after the other, culminating in possible kidney problems. My children rushed me to the hospital on June 16. It was very clear to the emergency doctor that I was also suffering from the loss of my mother. He asked me if I wanted to stay overnight, I said yes, and I was attached to IV and wheeled to a room.

I was so sad to find myself run down and in obvious pain, but the grief lingered on. Now my depression worsened, as I realized that not only was I having physical problems, but I missed my children terribly.

There was no end to it, all this misery, and I asked to see a chaplain for guidance and spiritual healing.

That wonderful woman came to my bedside for three days.

I have always had a very strong belief in God and in the power of prayer. I don't go often to worship as much as I would like, but I find it very enriching, helpful, and fulfilling.

On the third day, my grief was overwhelming. I fought to stifle my sobs and tears, but they tore out of me.

It seemed like an hour or two had gone by when I looked up and noticed something advancing towards my cubicle separated by blue drapes. A gigantic white silvery wave was tilting in the air and it was about to wash over me. I instinctively ducked, expecting to be immediately soaked through and through.

Then nothing happened. I peeked out over my blanket to find that the wave in the air just above my bed had disappeared.

I stopped crying at once. I wasn't sure if I had been touched by an angel or had been enlightened by something from the heavens. But I knew it had to be powerful. I felt washed over with love. It was almost as if I could hear someone say, "You are loved, and you will be all right. Do not be sad anymore."

It literally took my breath away and I could not understand what exactly had happened to me. I grew quiet and contemplative.

I was silent for the next few hours, as I made preparations to go home, as my son was on his way to collect me. The hospital had discharged me.

Just in case this story has people wondering whether I had hallucinated this event or happening, let me tell you that I was only given plain Tylenol by the third day, as all the test results came back negative. I was under-nourished, nearly anemic, lacking in iron, but with no kidney stones whatsoever. The doctor was mystified.

I can only surmise what came to me was something mystical. I have thought this over, and I have told my friends and family about the giant wave that soared over my bed.

In my life I have had many paranormal events happen to me, and my gift of second sight only gets stronger.

Two years prior to this spectacular experience, I had seen a boy-spirit in my kitchen one night during an electrical storm. I have heard my deceased grandmother speak to me while on a visit to Wales.

Clairaudient and clairvoyant incidents continue to give me signs of all kinds.

Was it my mother, hearing my cries, and trying to comfort me?

I wonder if I will ever know.

Two Precognitive Dreams?

Dwight Whalen

What are dreams? Are they vividly recalled nonsense, or are they camouflaged messages of some sort? Do they make subjective sense once the dreamer has found the "key" to them?

Written records from the earliest of times attest to the fact that men and women and children dreamt through the ages. For the last three hundred years, dream books have been popular. These are dictionaries, except that rather than explain the meaning of a given word, they offer a sense of its significance in the life of the dreamer. If you dream of finding a treasure, it may mean that you fear the absence of wealth, or it may mean that you anticipate the acquisition of it.

At the turn of the last century, Sigmund Freud made a signal contribution to the study of dreams when he published his study of the interpretation of dreams. This was the first full-length consideration of dreaming as an expression of human nature, rather than as a warning from the gods or as a vision of the future. He argued that dreams are "the guardians of sleep" and are produced by the subconscious to keep the subject sound asleep — entertained, puzzled — while the body proceeds to rejuvenate itself through the night, prior to the dawn of the new day. Freud also saw dreams as ways of entertaining thoughts that would normally be censored by the conscious mind during the day. At night they are given free play.

Again, are dreams precognitive, that is, predictive of future events? Dwight Whalen is inclined to answer "Yes." In this email, which I received on March 15, 2010, he has graphically described an instance in which a vivid dream that he entertained — or that entertained him — "came true" in an odd way.

Dwight is a long-time friend who lives in Niagara Falls, Ontario. He has become a popular historian of "the mighty cataract" and also of events of a psychical or paranormal nature. He pays attention to the contents of his dreams, and he seems puzzled when dream events correspond — or seem to correspond — to events that take place in his everyday life. Is there a causal connection or only a casual connection between the happenings that take place in the state of sleep and the happenings that take place in the world we share? Undoubtedly, there is one genuine connection and that connection is Dwight himself. In some manner still unrecognized, is he able to establish a connection between what he dreamt last night and what will occur tomorrow? Maybe. I will allow the reader to decide.

Hi, John:

I recall you keep a dream journal. Maybe I should, too. At least, I should make a mental note before falling to sleep each night to remember my dreams upon awakening. I've learned that without that intention present at sleep-time, whatever dreams I experience usually slip into oblivion on awakening.

About a week ago, I dreamed a peculiarly vivid (and peculiar) dream: I was watching a rock band perform, when suddenly one of the band members walked off stage and dropped dead in the wings. The scene was quickly followed by another, the appearance of TV-host Peter Marshall. He was addressing an audience, and a white-haired fellow stood off behind him to his right. Suddenly, Marshall began to have difficulty speaking. A woman whom I took to be a doctor entered the scene, holding a large syringe. Marshall struggled to speak, and managed to ask, "What is that for?" She replied, "It's okay, I'm putting you to sleep." Then she inserted the needle into his neck, and Marshall lost consciousness. He was "put to sleep," I knew, only in the sense a veterinarian puts an animal to sleep. He was dead, and there my dream ended.

Even without any pre-sleep intention, I recalled this dream easily when I woke, it was so vivid and disturbing. I pondered what it could mean, and later shared the dream with my friend Sue, who was as baffled as I. A number of things stood out for me in the dream — band music, sudden death, Peter Marshall, a doctor or nurse with a needle. Nothing preceding my sleep that night, or in the days beforehand, as far as I can recall, would have suggested to me any of these images, at least not consciously. I wondered if the dream might be, in some way, precognitive.

This afternoon, I was surfing TV channels and hit upon a show on WNED in Buffalo. It was program featuring music from the Big Band era — hosted by Peter Marshall. I was taken aback, recalling elements of my recent dream as I watched. Here were musicians performing, here was Marshall addressing an audience of TV viewers. Also, just as in my dream, off to his right was a second figure, a white-haired co-host whose full name escapes me now (Rosemary Clooney's brother). I continued to watch, slightly amazed, and with a touch of apprehension: While I knew that neither Marshall nor anybody else on the show was about to drop dead before my eyes, I wondered if the death element that featured so prominently in my dream was about to manifest in some other way — hoping, naturally, that I wasn't the one about to keel over!

No doubt it was with that thought in mind, and being concerned about my need to lose weight, that I decided it would be a good idea to go out for a long walk just then and burn off a few calories. As I was preparing to leave the house, and with the TV music still playing in the background, the phone rang. It was an acquaintance calling to tell me that the father of my late friend Rob Bracken had passed away in a nursing home. Death, as in my dream, had caught up with Peter Marshall and band music.

It seems to me that three of my dream's outstanding features — band music, death, and Peter Marshall — were precognitive hits, with a fourth, I suppose, being the white-haired co-host. In my dream, the band was a rock band, not an orchestra, but I don't know if that distinction is especially significant — even though it's unspeakably significant musically. Give me Glenn Miller over The Beatles any day! As for Rob's father, I can't imagine he was deliberately "put down" by a doctor or nurse. However, the phone call contained news of death in a facility one can easily associate with nurses and needles. A hit or a miss, take your pick.

Dreams certainly can be precognitive. The weight of human testimony affirms it, and my own personal experience concurs. Have you ever had a similar experience? Someday I'll relate to you another dream I had long ago that came true literally, in every last particular, a dream that left no doubt in my mind that future events can be foretold in dreams, however rarely this may happen. When it does, sometimes a future event is revealed in stark detail, and unfolds precisely as dreamed. More often, precognitive dream imagery, like dream imagery generally, speaks in symbols whose meaning is usually difficult or impossible to decipher, unless a later happening makes a reasonable interpretation possible, as in the dream related above.

I know you're a firm skeptic about things paranormal, more so than I am. I try to balance curiosity with healthy skepticism, walking a high-wire above the hard surfaces of True Belief on the one hand and "Skeptomania" on the other. (A skeptic is somebody who didn't see the ghost you did, and already doesn't like you.) We agree that people's experiences of the paranormal are usually true as experienced, as told too, but not necessarily true in the literal, objective sense.

Which gets back to dreams: obviously they are true as experienced; the question is, can they also at times be precognitive, and thus both subjective *and* objective? My personal experience is that they can. They can literally foretell an objective reality.

And oh yes — I did go for that walk.

Pleasant dreams,
Dwight

But that was not the end of it. I responded with alacrity to Dwight's letter, suggesting that some details of the dream may be interpreted but that others seemingly resist interpretation. Yet, dreams have a habit of returning or recurring, and so do accounts of them. Dwight sent to me a second email.

John:

Thanks so much for your feedback about my dream. You've given me something else to ponder. I agree with the statement you quoted about the world of dreams being one of both nonsense and, to coin a word, *supersense*. Excellent.

Today, I read some of Judith Orloff's book, *Second Sight*, the story of her gift of intuition, her suppression of it in medical school, her struggle to embrace and develop it as a therapeutic aid in her psychiatric practice. I came upon a passage where she described a death scene, and naturally found it quite difficult to read.

Orloff's book is interesting, compassionate, and validating. Intuition, of course, is a knowing-without-the-how-of-knowing, if I may put it so clumsily. We all experience this on occasion. Most of us — I'm no different — tend to dismiss or minimize our intuitions, rationalizing them away, explaining them as the product of subtle cues that slipped past our conscious mind but resonate and communicate back to us from the subconscious. I've no doubt this happens — at least it sounds plausible — I'm just not persuaded there isn't something truly mysterious going on when we get feelings we can't explain. Or experience dreams that literally come true.

You asked me to share the other precognitive dream I mentioned. It occurred many years ago when I worked one summer as a city bus driver. Can you imagine me as a bus driver? Neither can I. One doesn't need to delve into the psychic to encounter the unexplained; looking into a mirror will often suffice! It was the worst job

I've ever had. No way was I cut out to be a bus driver. The stress was incredible, the work schedule gruelling. I toughed it out for two reasons: the pay was excellent, and I wanted to impress a girlfriend who'd dumped me. She was convinced I'd never be a good wage-earner and I was determined to prove her wrong, if only for one summer. Plus, I didn't want to see myself as a quitter. I wanted to prove I could be a good bus driver, that I could take whatever the job threw at me. So I endured ten weeks of living hell. Ten weeks and one day, to be exact.

Eventually, I reached a point where I didn't give a damn what my ex-girlfriend thought. All I wanted was to get my layoff notice, which I knew would be coming around Labour Day. Now, the precise manner in which I would be notified of my layoff wasn't something I'd given any thought to. Why would I? But had I thought of it at all, I would have guessed that I'd be sent a notice in the mail, or the boss would call me into his office, or I'd get a pink slip with my pay cheque — obvious scenarios like that.

One night I had the following dream: I walked into the bus driver's lunchroom at City Hall. I was alone in the room. In the centre of the table was a neat stack of white letter-sized envelopes, four in all, the number of seasonal bus drivers hired that summer. I picked up the stack and noticed a typed name on the front of each envelope. In alphabetical order, they were the names of the four summer bus drivers. "Whalen" was the fourth envelope. I knew without opening it that it contained my layoff notice. Here the dream ended.

When I woke, I didn't consider the dream precognitive. In spite of my life-long interest in non-ordinary perception and knowing, I regarded the dream as an example of wish fulfillment. I hated my job so much, wanted my layoff so desperately, my sub-conscious mind was "venting" to relieve painful emotional stress, concocting a scenario that I didn't regard as precognitive, merely bizarre, in keeping with the confounding nature of dreams. That's how I interpreted it. Never would I have imagined receiving my layoff notice in such an unorthodox way. Obviously, it was "only a dream." I didn't share my dream with anybody.

One day, about a week later, as Labour Day neared, I pulled my bus into a stop near City Hall and got off for my lunch break. The driver who relieved me said, "Your layoff notice is in the lunch room." Instantly I recalled my "non-precognitive" dream, and each step I took toward the City Hall building was slow and deliberate. Shall I cut-and-paste from the dream paragraph above? The lunch-room was empty, four white envelopes were neatly stacked in the middle of the table, the name of a summer bus driver typed on each, all placed in alphabetical order, with "Whalen" on the bottom. I opened mine and it was indeed my layoff notice. My lunch that day included much food for thought.

Dwight

IN THE DIMNESS WAS A LITTLE GIRL

Randy L. Whynacht

I received an email on October 15, 2008, from Randy L. Whynacht. He identified himself as a purchaser of my latest publication at the time, *The Big Book of Canadian Ghost Stories*. In his email, he drew my attention to his blog and suggested that I would find it interesting. He was right. I did find it interesting, and with his permission I am reproducing its account of a mysterious experience in the present book.

Mr. Whynacht is a native of Lunenburg who resides with his "incomparable wife Diana" and their three dogs outside Bridgewater, Nova Scotia. He is president of Whynacht Security & Survival. Here is how his company is described: "Whynacht Security & Survival is a proudly Nova Scotian company that has been applying its unique, effective and proven approach to the providing of protection and peace of mind for thousands of clients since 1983."

I have titled his account "In the Dimness Was a Little Girl." The reader will find it to be written with clarity and care, as well as concern, so the experience is vividly recounted and quite graphic. I have no ready explanation for what happened.

In 1984 I moved into a large house on Lincoln Street in Lunenburg. The layout of the stairway to the second floor prevented me from taking my bed frame up to the master bedroom, so I had to sleep on the mattress on the floor as a stopgap measure.

On the first night I slept in the house, fagged out with the toils inherent in moving, I crawled under the sheets, my faithful beagle-spaniel mutt Jasper curled up at the foot of my makeshift bed.

Jasper had a very low growl. Almost inaudible, and he was sparing in its use. Nevertheless, it was the sound of his growl that woke me. Opening my eyes and raising my head to look down at him, I could see his silhouette against the wall. He was looking straight at the bedroom door, which was to my left, and a ball of fur was raised on his shoulders. When I looked at the doorway I saw why he was growling.

What I saw in the dimness was a little girl, I would guess about five or six years old, standing in the doorway, smiling at me. She had long hair and was wearing a plaid jumper with an old-timey cut. When our eyes met and I registered what I was seeing, I yelled, "Hey!" and quickly began to get off the mattress. At this point I really felt I was looking at a child.

I heard her giggle and saw her run off. In the five or so seconds it took me to get to my feet, pull on my robe (she was a kid after all), and reach my bedroom door, the little girl had gone to stand grinning mischievously at me from the doorway of another bedroom across the landing.

"Wait!" I called as I moved toward her. She stepped inside the room and I saw the door begin to close, but it wasn't quite shut when I reached it.

Tired and getting irritated at incompetent parents who let their kids run riot through strange houses in the middle of the night, I grabbed the door and pushed it ahead of me as I started to enter the room. Suddenly I felt the door stop as though it had hit a solid obstruction, and then it flew back at me. The edge of the door hit me in the forehead and the impact threw me backwards onto the landing.

Now really pissed off, I went back and kicked the door fully open. There was no resistance this time, and my strike threw the door open hard enough for the doorknob to break through the lathe and plaster wall as it impacted against it. Stepping into the room, I saw ... no one. The room was empty except for a couple of boxes I had placed there earlier in the day.

The next day I had a beautiful bruise on my forehead, and I checked with everyone I knew who had ever lived in that house to see if any of them had ever seen or heard of the mysterious little girl. Nobody had.

I never saw the little girl again, but to the end of his days, Jasper wouldn't enter that room, giving it a wide berth, and a suspicious look whenever he passed it.

Two Angels Watching over Me

Danielle Young

I received the following email on May 16, 2009. It deals with the ever-popular, ever-elusive subject of angels.

Dear Mr. Colombo:

Hi. My name is Danielle Young, and I live in Canada. I've read your book *Haunting Stories*. I have a story of my own, but it's not a haunting. I'm not quite sure if you'd be interested to hear it, but I can tell you that it is truthful. It happened to me, and I don't think I could of got through the bad circumstances which I was in without it. If you want to hear more of what I have to say, please feel free to respond.

Thanks,
Danielle Young

I immediately responded and said, in effect, "Yes, I would like to read your story." The next day, I received the account that appears here.

Here, I will add only the fact that the experience described by Ms. Young is not at all unusual. While she was *in extremis*, her fears were alleviated by a vision of two people and by a message that all would come out well in the end. The two people were deceased loved ones, in effect, "guardian angels."

I was born in Brampton, Ontario. But in the summer of 1990, when I was five, we moved to St. John's, Newfoundland.

December 20, 1999, when I was fourteen years old, I was in a very bad car accident. I suffered very serious head and leg injuries and was in a coma for three weeks. When I woke up, my speech was slurred to the point nobody could understand me. I also had to learn to walk again.

I don't recall how long after I woke up that I first saw my Nan. When I was in the hospital, my Mom wrote notes to me that filled two exercise books. She said I once asked her to move out of the way because she was blocking my view of my Nan and Pop. She told me I used to have conversations with Nan.

I saw my Pop when I was younger, but by the time I had moved, he had died. I'm sure I did, but I don't ever remember seeing him. My short-term memory is not all that good. But repetition helps.

The last time I saw both Nan and Pop was when I was in the hospital. They told me they loved me and that I'd be okay. Then they walked away, hand in hand, which was of some comfort because my Nan had used a cane.

I knew that they had helped me wake up, and were still in a way pushing me to get better, and not give up. Maybe the point of them appearing to me then was to reassure me things would be all right. I really couldn't think of two better people to deliver the news.

I know that to other people this story may not seem significant, but it means the world to me. Now I know for sure I have two angels watching over me.

A Note from the Author

I urge readers to contact me should they wish to share their odd experiences or unusual events with my future readers. I may be reached in three ways.

Readers may write to me care of the editorial department of Dundurn; the publishing house's address appears on the copyright page. They may send their emails to jrc@colombo.ca. Or they may contact me through my website, *www.colombo.ca*, which includes an essay on the nature of the unknown, on anomalous experiences, and on the mysteries of Canada in particular.

The Big Book of Canadian Hauntings

978-1554884490

$29.99

The Big Book of Canadian Hauntings offers readers true, first-person accounts of the appearances (and the disappearances!) of ghosts and spirits, as well as considerations and discussions of their effects on observers. Some told-as-true tales are reprinted from newspapers and periodicals of the past, but the majority of the stories, which come from every region in Canada, are based on eyewitness reports of the present that appear here for the first time. Whether you believe in ghosts, spirits, spooks, spectres, or poltergeists, or not, after reading these narratives contributed by Canadians from all walks of life, you definitely won't be indifferent to them.

Available at your favourite bookseller.

www.dundurn.com

What did you think of this book?
Visit *www.dundurn.com* for reviews, videos, updates, and more!

Also by John Robert Colombo

Fascinating Canada
A Book of Questions and Answers
978-1554889235
$19.99

Fascinating Canada is the product of over half a century of research, reading, writing, and thinking. Here is a book about the Canadian past, present, and future. The information in *Fascinating Canada* is organized under four headings (People, Places, Things, Ideas), and there is a detailed Index for ready reference. This book may serve as a work of popular reference, but it has been written to stimulate inquiry and spark a sense of surprise in the minds of readers who know something about this amazing country, but perhaps not as much as the author. Open this book and begin to read ... and match wits with author and researcher John Robert Colombo.

The Big Book of Canadian Ghost Stories
978-1550028447
$29.99

Here are Canada's haunted houses, ghosts and polter-geists, weird visions of the past and improbable visions of the future, and assurances that there is life after death. Included are more than 175 accounts of such events and experiences told mainly by the witnesses themselves — Canadians from all walks of life and all parts of the country. Some of the stories are classics. Others are little known. About one-third of the accounts have never before appeared in print. Whatever your views are about the supernatural and the paranormal — skeptic, believer, middle-of-the-road — this huge collection of stories filled with thrills and chills will cause you to wonder about the nature of human life and the afterlife.